Black Historical Figures

MUSICIANS

Copyright © 2023 by Every Dollar Countz LLC
All rights reserved. This book or any portion thereof
may not be reproduced or used in any manner whatsoever
without the express written permission of the publisher
except for the use of brief quotations in a book review.

TABLE OF CONTENTS

195 RIHANNA

43 MICHAEL JACKSON

67 WHITNEY HOUSTON

3 Aretha Franklin	67 Whitney Houston	131 Ethel Waters
11 Louis Armstrong	75 O'Shea Jackson Sr.	139 Will Smith
19 Aaliyah	83 Ella Fitzgerald	147 Anita Baker
27 Dizzy Gillespie	91 Miles Davis	155 Nasir bin Olu Dara Jones
35 Billie Holiday	99 Diana Ross	163 Pearl Bailey
43 Michael Jackson	107 Shawn Carter	171 Beyonce' Knowles
51 Nina Simone	115 Hazel Scott	179 Miriam Makeba
59 Tupac Amaru Shakur	123 Lawrence Parker	187 Marian Anderson
		195 Robyn Rihanna Fenty

These Workbooks are geared to intrigue, inspire and motivate you to want to learn more about these Black Historical Figures(BHFs) and others. Also to do more research on your own. We know this isn't all the history of these individuals. We want you to do some of the research also. We try to be as accurate as possible during our research. If there are some stories or questions that aren't as stated, please contact us at info@wegonnalearntoday.com.

Aretha Franklin

Aretha Franklin

March 25, 1942 – August 16, 2018
SINGER

3

LEFT BLANK ON PURPOSE

Aretha Franklin

Aretha Franklin

Aretha Franklin

Aretha Franklin

Aretha Franklin

Directions: read the bio below and answer the following questions.

Hi, my name is Aretha Franklin. I was born on March 25, 1942, in Memphis, TN. I signed my first recording deal at 14 with J.V.B. Records. In 1956, my first single, "Never Grow Old," was released. It was from my album "Spirituals". When I was 16, I went on tour with Dr. Martin Luther King, Jr. and I sang at his funeral in 1968. I was signed with Columbia from 1960–1966. My first single to chart on the Billboard Hot 100, "Won't Be Long," which was on my first album, "Aretha: With the Ray Bryant Combo", peaked at number 7 on the RGB chart. In the 1960s some were already calling me "the Queen of Soul." Some of my best years and hits came when I signed with Atlantic Records (1966–1979). Some of the hits that came from that era were "I Never Loved a Man (The Way I Love You)," "Respect," "Do Right Woman, Do Right Man," "Chain of Fools," "Ain't No Way," "Think," and "I Say a Little Prayer," to name a few. I was the first female performer to be inducted into the Rock and Roll Hall of Fame.

1. How old was I when I signed with J.V.B. Records?
   A. 16
   B. 12
   C. 14
2. What year did I sign with Atlantic Records?
   A. 1966
   B. 1960
   C. 1968
3. I was the first female performer to what?
   A. Get inducted into the Musicians Hall of Fame
   B. Get inducted into the Rock and Roll Hall of Fame
   C. Get inducted into America's Pop Music Hall of Fame

Directions: Answer the questions, to solve the crossword puzzle. You can use the internet if you get stuck on any question.

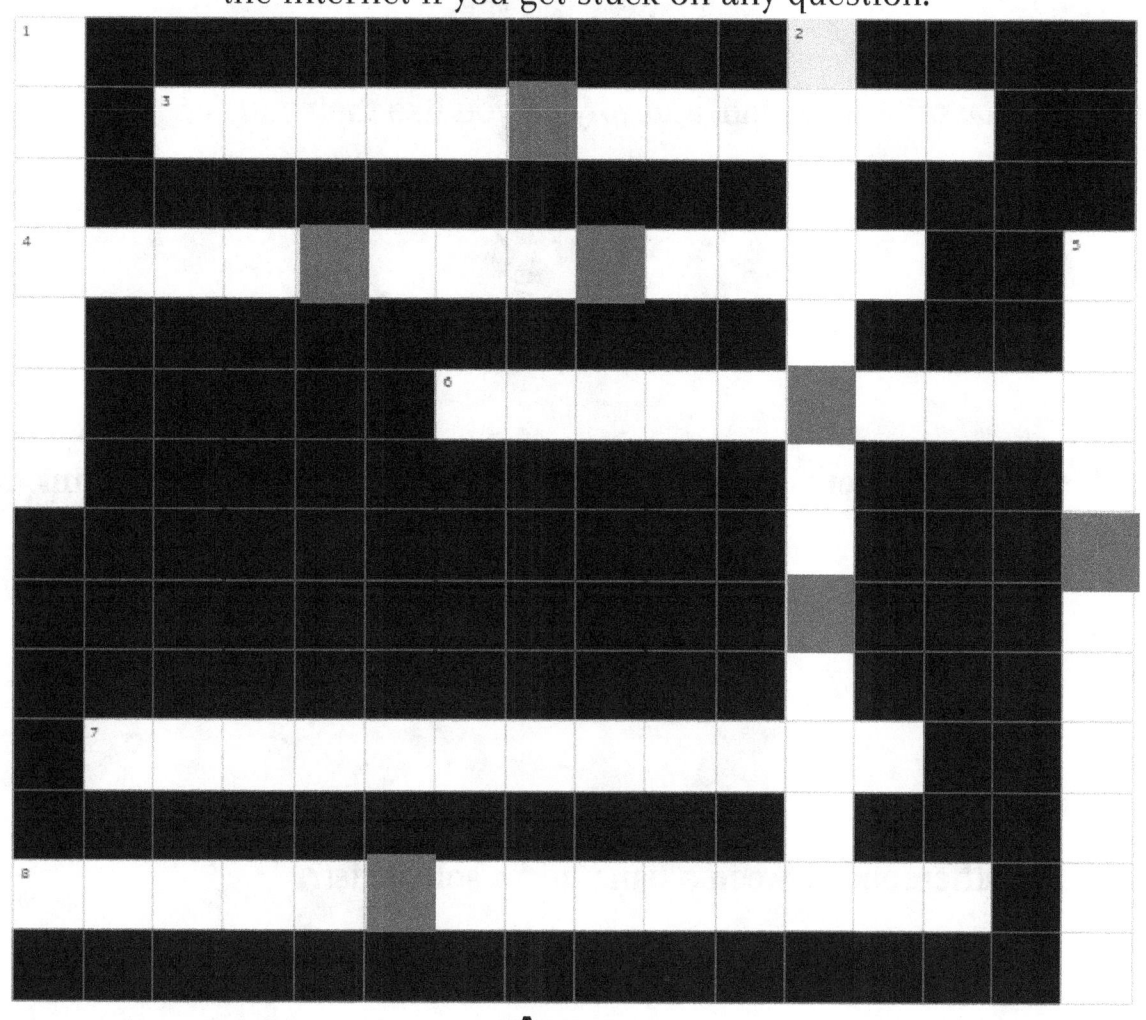

Across

3) Aretha was active in the fight for _____ and women's rights.
4) Aretha was the first female performer inducted into the _____ Hall of Fame.
6) Aretha performed "The Star-Spangled Banner" with Aaron Neville and Dr. John for _____ XL.
7) Aretha received the _____ Medal of Freedom.
8) Aretha played herself in the movie The _____.

Down

1) Aretha is the most _____ female artist in history as of 2022.
2) Aretha was inducted into the National Women's_____.
5) Aretha was a _____ musician who learned to play the piano by ear and couldn't read music.

Directions: Read and answer the questions. These are your opinions so the answers will vary.

Who is your favorite musician, and why do you like their music?

What kind of instruments do musicians play, and which one do you think is the hardest to learn?

What is the difference between a band and a solo artist?

Directions: Unscramble the words below about Aretha. See if you can get the bonus word.

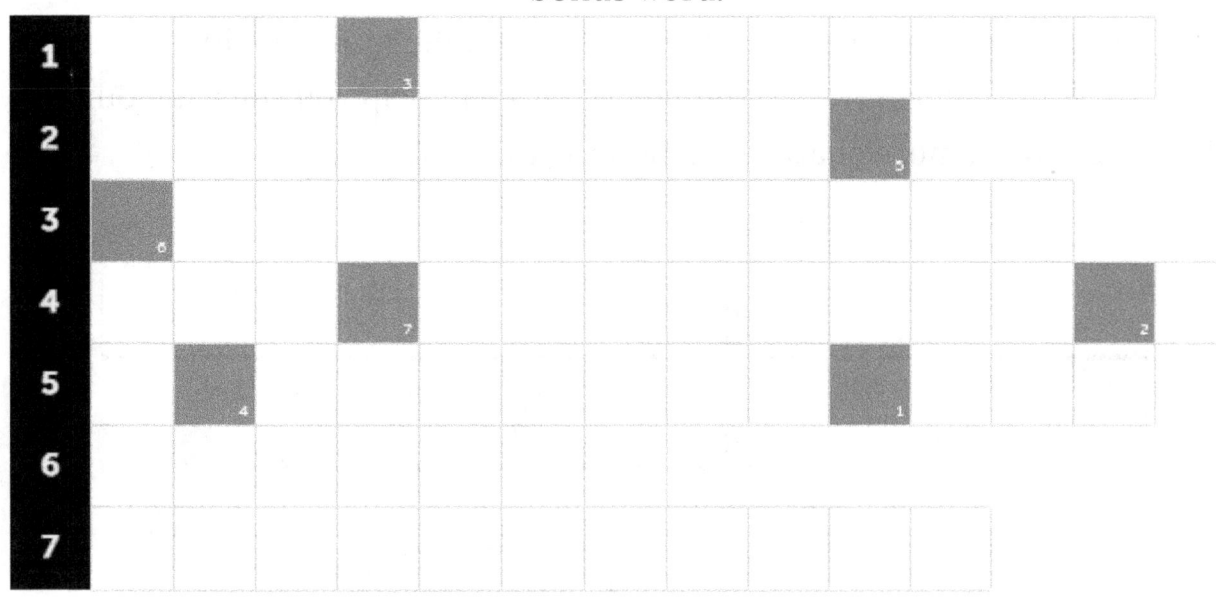

BONUS WORD

Unscramble Words

1) aedtscrrosira   **2)** falmflaoeh   **3)** ifanhocsolof
4) enlytmahrbushd **5)** apahheslrnism **6)** pemsmhi
7) oeuufenqsol

Directions: This is the WGLT Challenge. Solve the cryptogram. As the puzzle solver, you need to find which number belongs to which character. And this can be pretty challenging! You will need to match the number with the letter. There are some letters given to you below. This will help you solve the other words and unlock more characters. **Good Luck.**

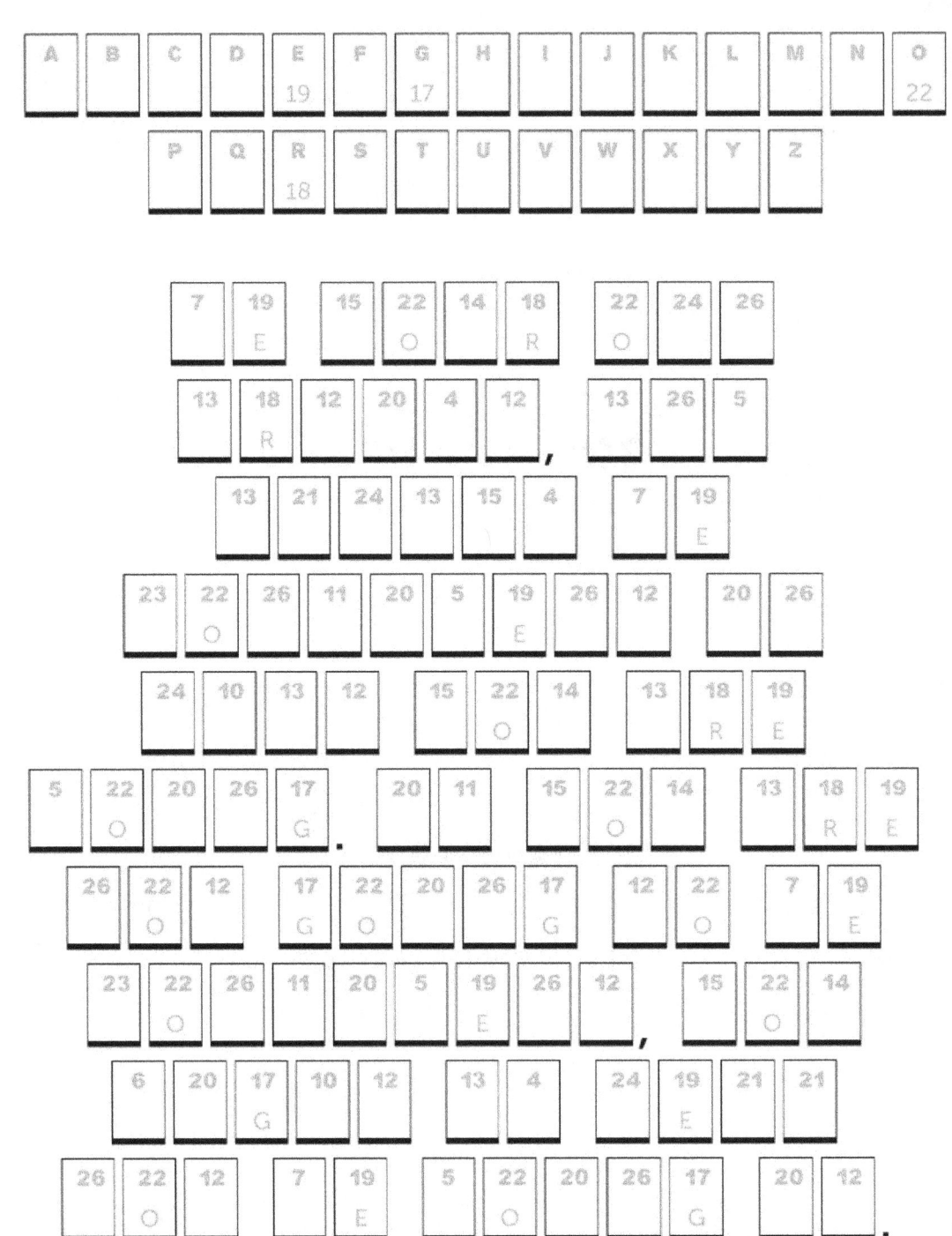

Louis Armstrong

Louis Armstrong

August 4, 1901 – July 6, 1971
TRUMPETER AND VOCALIST

LEFT BLANK ON PURPOSE

Louis Armstrong

Louis Armstrong

Louis Armstrong

Louis Armstrong

Louis Armstrong

Louis Armstrong

Directions: read the bio below and answer the following questions.

Hi, my name is Louis Armstrong. I was born on August 4, 1901, in New Orleans, LA. I dropped out of school when I was 11. I worked for the Karnoffskies, who were Jewish. I wore a Star of David in memory of this family who had raised me. I joined a quartet of boys and we sang in the streets for money. I learned to play by ear at Dago Tony's honkytonk. Every time I closed my eyes while blowing that trumpet of mine, I felt like I was looking right into the heart of good old New Orleans. It gave me something to live for. One of the things I'm best known for is that I was requested for a royal performance. We got ready to play "You Rascal, You." Without warning or permission, I looked straight up at the monarch and hollered, "This one's for you, Rex!" Some of the songs that I'm known for are "What a Wonderful World," "All of Me," "Hello Dolly," "I'm in the Mood for Love," and "Love, You Funny Thing." I use to be called "Dippermouth," "Gatemouth," and "Satchelmouth." But, while I was in England, they abbreviated it by calling me "Satchmo." That came to be a part of my name.

1. How did I learn to play the trumpet?
    A. Music teacher
    B. Church
    C. By ear
2. What nickname stuck with me thru the years?
    A. Dippermouth
    B. Satchmo
    C. Satchelmouth
3. What city is in my heart every time I play the trumpet?
    A. Chicago
    B. Jacksonville
    C. New Orleans

Directions: Find the words associated with Louis's life and career.

V	H	S	D	D	T	B	T	G	L	V	N	B	V	L	Q	S	D
S	A	M	J	V	J	N	R	H	J	F	O	V	P	S	X	E	V
T	R	Z	W	A	S	Y	T	L	P	C	V	X	H	J	C	B	Z
A	L	F	A	S	Z	P	G	R	W	J	S	Q	G	C	I	W	F
R	E	K	Z	T	M	Z	O	N	W	C	R	B	A	A	O	R	I
O	M	I	R	B	H	Y	A	P	I	E	S	R	A	O	R	W	P
F	R	N	L	I	X	U	L	S	T	G	E	C	R	D	H	B	
D	E	D	G	W	D	E	M	E	A	C	N	E	A	T	Y	K	D
A	N	K	X	V	U	Q	P	L	O	D	J	I	J	N	J	T	Z
V	A	Z	J	X	X	M	N	R	O	Q	Z	R	S	P	E	L	R
I	I	H	W	K	U	A	D	G	A	U	D	D	D	T	S	L	S
D	S	K	D	R	P	S	K	S	P	M	I	M	P	V	A	E	O
L	S	K	T	X	Q	T	M	T	N	A	F	S	J	G	V	C	W
Y	A	J	V	X	J	K	Z	M	H	C	Y	N	I	I	O	T	S
Q	N	Y	T	E	I	C	O	S	H	G	I	H	F	A	I	K	K
O	C	Q	T	Q	G	A	H	P	R	Y	C	T	H	Z	N	C	R
U	E	O	K	J	C	V	Z	E	Q	V	O	G	W	F	A	F	
P	B	G	U	X	C	K	Q	C	Q	H	F	E	F	S	G	C	S

Find These Words

POPS TRUMPETER JAZZ
LOUISIANA HIGHSOCIETY STAROFDAVID
HOTFIVE HARLEMRENAISSANCE SCATSINGING
DECCARECORDS

Directions: Read and answer the questions. These are your opinions so the answers will vary.

Can you name some famous musicians from different time periods and genres?

What is a concert, and have you ever been to one?

What is your favorite song, and who is the musician that performs it?

Directions: Read and answer the questions below. There are clues in the puzzle to help you. Try and solve the cryptic message.

Clue for cryptic message: One of Louis's nicknames.

Questions

1) Louis served as a "musical _____" for the U.S. State Department.

2) Louis's second wife pushed him to step out on his own which led to him recording his first solo _____.

3) Louis _____ New Orleans until they lifted the ban prohibiting integrated bands.

4) Louis gave King George V a new _____, which was Rex.

5) Louis got his first ___ from the Jewish family he worked for.

6) Louis wore a Star of David pendant to honor the Jewish family who fed and _____ him.

7) Louis's song "What a _____ World" didn't make the Billboard charts till it was included in the soundtrack of the Robin Williams film "Good Morning, Vietnam."

17

Directions: This is the WGLT Challenge. Solve the cryptogram. As the puzzle solver, you need to find which number belongs to which character. And this can be pretty challenging! You will need to match the number with the letter. There are some letters given to you below. This will help you solve the other words and unlock more characters. **Good Luck.**

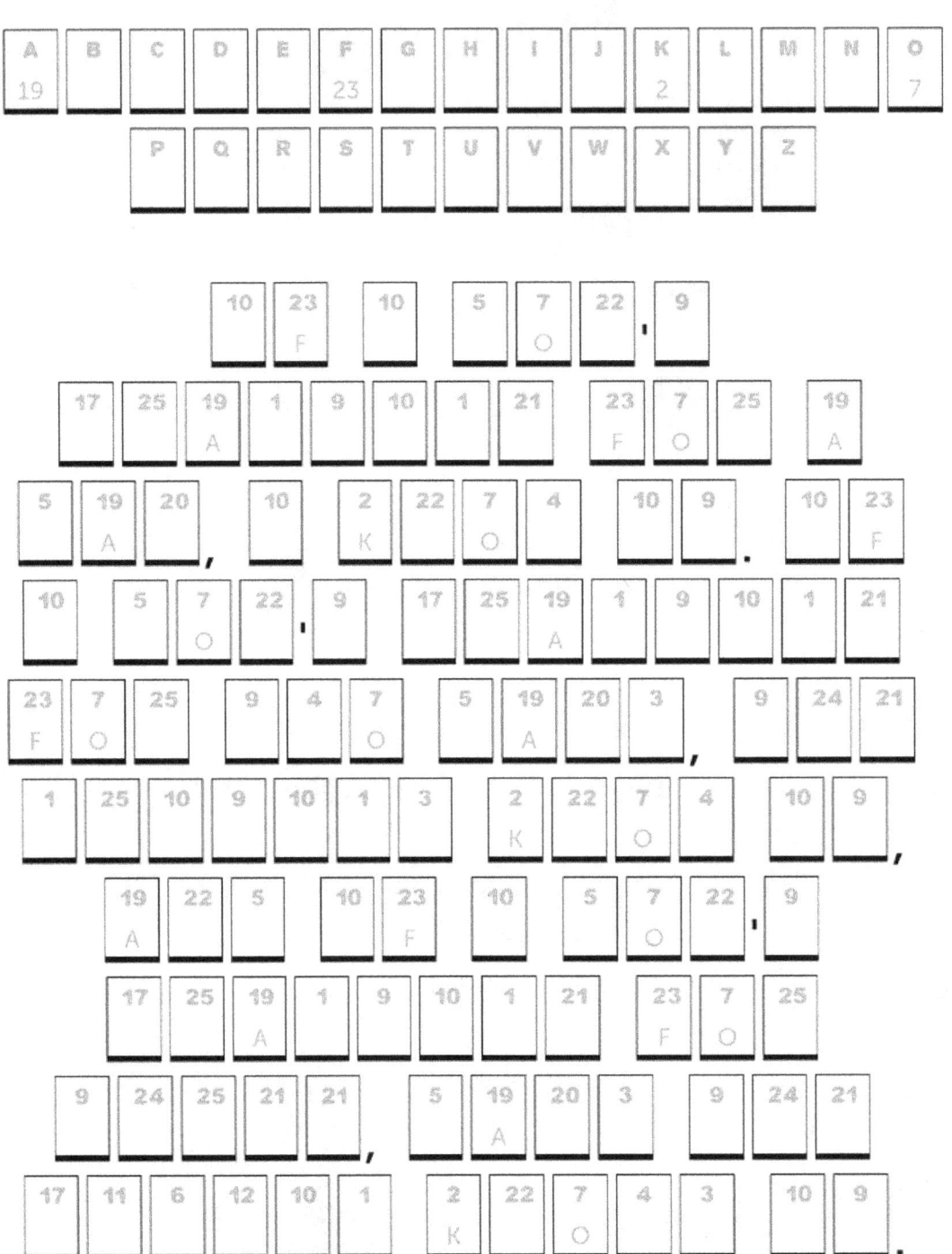

18

January 16, 1979 – August 25, 2001
SINGER/ACTRESS

19

Aaliyah Dana Haughton

Aaliyah Dana Haughton

Aaliyah Dana Haughton

Aaliyah Dana Haughton

Aaliyah Dana Haughton

Aaliyah Dana Haughton

Directions: read the bio below and answer the following questions.

Hi, my name is Aaliyah Haughton. I was born on January 16, 1979, in Brooklyn, NY. I graduated from the Detroit High School for the Fine and Performing Arts. I was on Star Search when I was 10. I performed with Gladys Knight at some of her concerts. I signed with my uncle Barry Hankerson's label, Blackground Records, when I was 12. He introduced me to R. Kelly and in 1994, I released my first album, Age Ain't Nothing but a Number. The album went double platinum. In 1996, I went to Atlantic Records. I worked with record producers Timbaland and Missy Elliott, who helped me with my second studio album, One in a Million. It also went double platinum. In 1999, I was in my first film, Romeo Must Die. I was also the executive producer for the movie's soundtrack. I contributed four tracks to the soundtrack. My song "Try Again" topped the Billboard Hot 100, which made me the first artist to top the chart based solely on airplay. Some of the songs I'm known for are "One in a Million," "Are You That Somebody," and "Rock the Boat".

1. Who did I perform with when I was younger?
    A. Gladys Knight
    B. Michael Jackson
    C. Whitney Houston
2. How old was I when I signed my first record deal?
    A. 14
    B. 13
    C. 12
3. My first film I was in was?
    A. Queen of the Damned
    B. Romeo Must Die
    C. New York Undercover

Directions: Answer the questions, to solve the crossword puzzle. You can use the internet if you get stuck on any question.

Across

1) Aaliyah debut album, Age Ain't Nothing but a Number was certified _____ at that time.

6) Aaliyah was dating co-founder of Roc-A-Fella Records _____ before she passed away.

7) Aaliyah's vocal range was of a _____.

8) Aaliyah was the spokesperson for the _____ Corporation.

Down

2) Aaliyah was the youngest singer to perform at the _____ at that time.

3) Aaliyah was _____ by a number of performers like Michael Jackson, Stevie Wonder and Sade to name a few.

4) Aaliyah covered her left eye off the advice of her _____.

5) Aaliyah _____ a 4.0 grade point average in high school while managing her career.

Directions: Read and answer the questions. These are your opinions so the answers will vary.

How do musicians create music, and what does it take to write a song?

_____
_____

Can you explain what a music video is, and have you seen any before?

_____
_____

What is your favorite genre of music, and can you name some musicians who perform in that genre?

_____
_____
_____
_____

Directions: Unscramble the words below about Aaliyah. See if you can get the bonus word.

BONUS WORD

Unscramble Words

1) ainldtbma
2) nnnlmieialoio
3) mmyrawraagd
4) otsiyiseltlm
5) riuooemetmds
6) rsharcseta
7) broppnau
8) ocrknaahdftb

Directions: This is the WGLT Challenge. Solve the cryptogram. As the puzzle solver, you need to find which number belongs to which character. And this can be pretty challenging! You will need to match the number with the letter. There are some letters given to you below. This will help you solve the other words and unlock more characters. **Good Luck.**

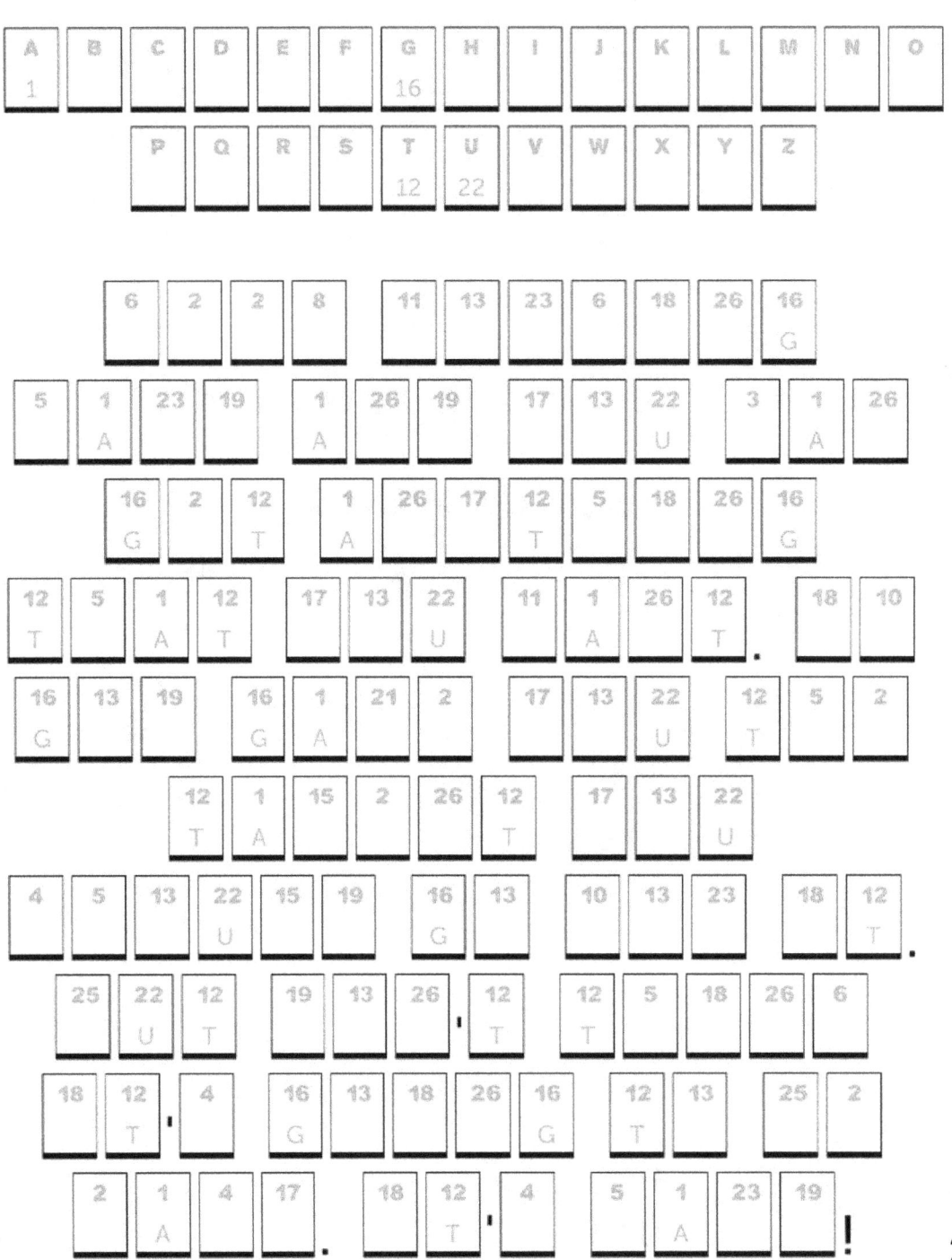

26

John Birks Gillespie

John Birks Gillespie

October 21, 1917 – January 6, 1993
JAZZ TRUMPETER 27

LEFT BLANK ON PURPOSE

John Birks Gillespie

John Birks Gillespie

John Birks Gillespie

John Birks Gillespie

John Birks Gillespie

John Birks Gillespie

Directions: read the bio below and answer the following questions.

Hi, my name is John Gillespie. I was born on October 21, 1917, in Cheraw, SC. I started playing the piano when I was 4 and taught myself the trombone and trumpet by the age of 12. I won a music scholarship to the Laurinburg Institute in North Carolina. I went there for a while then moved to Philadelphia in 1935. I got my first professional job with the Frank Fairfax Orchestra in 1935. I then joined the Edgar Hayes Orchestrate and later joined the Teddy Hill Orchestra. In 1939, I joined Cab Calloway's orchestra. I was known for clowning and being unpredictable, which earned me the nickname "Dizzy." In 1951, I founded a record label, Dee Gee Records, but it closed in 1953. In 1956, I organized a band to go on a State Department tour of the Middle East, which was well-received internationally and I earned the nickname "the Ambassador of Jazz." In 1964, I put myself forward as an independent write-in candidate for the United States presidential campaign. One of the things I'm best known for is developing the musical genre known as "bebop."

1. What instrument was I known for playing?
   A. Piano
   B. Trumpet
   C. Trombone
2. What year did I run for President?
   A. 1960
   B. 1968
   C. 1964
3. I was known as who during the State Department tour?
   A. Dizzy
   B. Mr. Gillespie
   C. Ambassador of Jazz

Directions: Find the words associated with Dizzy's life and career.

I	I	T	G	R	A	M	M	Y	A	W	A	R	D	S	C	T	I
G	G	R	O	T	A	C	U	D	E	O	E	M	M	C	I	Y	U
E	Q	B	B	U	H	L	R	H	O	X	E	N	G	L	A	Y	H
K	O	A	T	C	A	J	L	J	T	G	W	J	T	W	P	D	Y
J	P	N	P	K	R	F	H	D	S	W	H	N	S	G	B	M	G
Z	L	D	Q	Z	T	C	R	E	S	I	V	O	R	P	M	I	C
K	G	L	S	U	S	L	J	P	W	K	E	U	W	U	T	I	S
A	V	E	S	Z	E	A	E	I	N	Y	W	M	M	K	H	R	L
U	M	A	W	Q	H	Y	Q	Q	B	E	L	O	G	T	E	G	I
L	Q	D	E	A	C	C	N	E	S	H	R	P	U	R	R	D	Y
T	L	E	X	B	R	R	B	L	Z	O	X	W	X	U	F	U	I
R	U	R	P	V	O	O	V	B	E	Z	H	V	T	M	G	L	A
U	K	B	A	Z	P	W	W	Q	N	L	A	L	C	P	P	C	V
P	O	D	D	E	D	I	G	F	I	C	B	J	L	E	Z	L	M
V	I	C	P	T	C	N	G	N	I	G	N	I	S	T	A	C	S
J	C	O	M	P	O	S	E	R	A	E	Z	K	R	E	T	X	N
A	M	K	T	I	U	K	X	X	J	R	I	M	D	R	V	N	L
M	Z	V	J	L	S	N	A	E	Z	P	R	S	N	Y	H	A	I

Find These Words

IMPROVISER ORCHESTRA TRUMPETER
BEBOP JAZZ BANDLEADER
EDUCATOR COMPOSER GRAMMYAWARDS
SCATSINGING

Directions: Read and answer the questions. These are your opinions so the answers will vary.

How do musicians practice their craft, and what does it take to become a successful musician?

Who is your favorite musician and why?

What instruments do musicians play?

Directions: Read and answer the questions below. There are clues in the puzzle to help you. Try and solve the cryptic message.

Clue for cryptic message: Dizzy was considered to be this.

Questions

1) Dizzy was a major figure in the _____ of bebop and modern jazz.
2) Dizzy starred in the _____ The Winter in Lisbon.
3) Dizzy first professional job was with the Frank Fairfax _____ in 1935.
4) Dizzy _____ trumpet featured a bell which bent upward at a 45-degree angle rather than pointing straight ahead as in the conventional design.
5) Dizzy joined the Earl Hines band 'the _____ of bop' in 1943.
6) Dizzy pioneered _____-Cuban jazz.
7) Dizzy made his first recording, "King Porter _____". In August 1937.
8) Dizzy led the United Nations _____.

Directions: This is the WGLT Challenge. Solve the cryptogram. As the puzzle solver, you need to find which number belongs to which character. And this can be pretty challenging! You will need to match the number with the letter. There are some letters given to you below. This will help you solve the other words and unlock more characters. **Good Luck.**

Billie Holiday

Billie Holiday

April 7, 1915 – July 17, 1959
JAZZ AND SWING MUSIC SINGER

35

LEFT BLANK ON PURPOSE

Billie Holiday

Billie Holiday

Billie Holiday

Billie Holiday

Billie Holiday

Billie Holiday

Directions: read the bio below and answer the following questions.

Hi, my name is Eleanora Fagan. I was born on April 7, 1915, in Philadelphia, PA. I was 14 when I started singing in nightclubs in Harlem. I came up with my professional pseudonym by borrowing the last name of an actress I admired and using my dad's performing name, Billie Dove. I was discovered by producer Joh Hammond when I was 18. John liked how I sang like an improvising jazz genius. I recorded my first record in 1933. I was in the film Symphony in Black with Duke Ellington. In 1938, I was the first Black woman to work with a white orchestra. I debuted "Strange Fruit" during a 1939 performance at Cafe Society, which was New York's first integrated nightclub. In 1947, I was in the movie New Orleans with my idol, Louis Armstrong. I performed at Carnegie Hall in 1948, where I had three curtain calls before a sold-out crowd. Some of the songs I'm known for are "Strange Fruit," "Fine and Mellow," "The Man I Love," "Billie's Blues," "God Bless the Child," and "I Wished on the Moon."

1. Where did I debut my hit song Strange Fruit?
    A. Carnegie Hall
    B. Cafe Society
    C. Cotton Club
2. How old was I when I started singing in night clubs?
    A. 18
    B. 15
    C. 14
3. I was the first African American woman to what?
    A. Perform with a white singer
    B. Perform with a white orchestra
    C. Perform with a white pianist

Directions: Answer the questions, to solve the crossword puzzle. You can use the internet if you get stuck on any question.

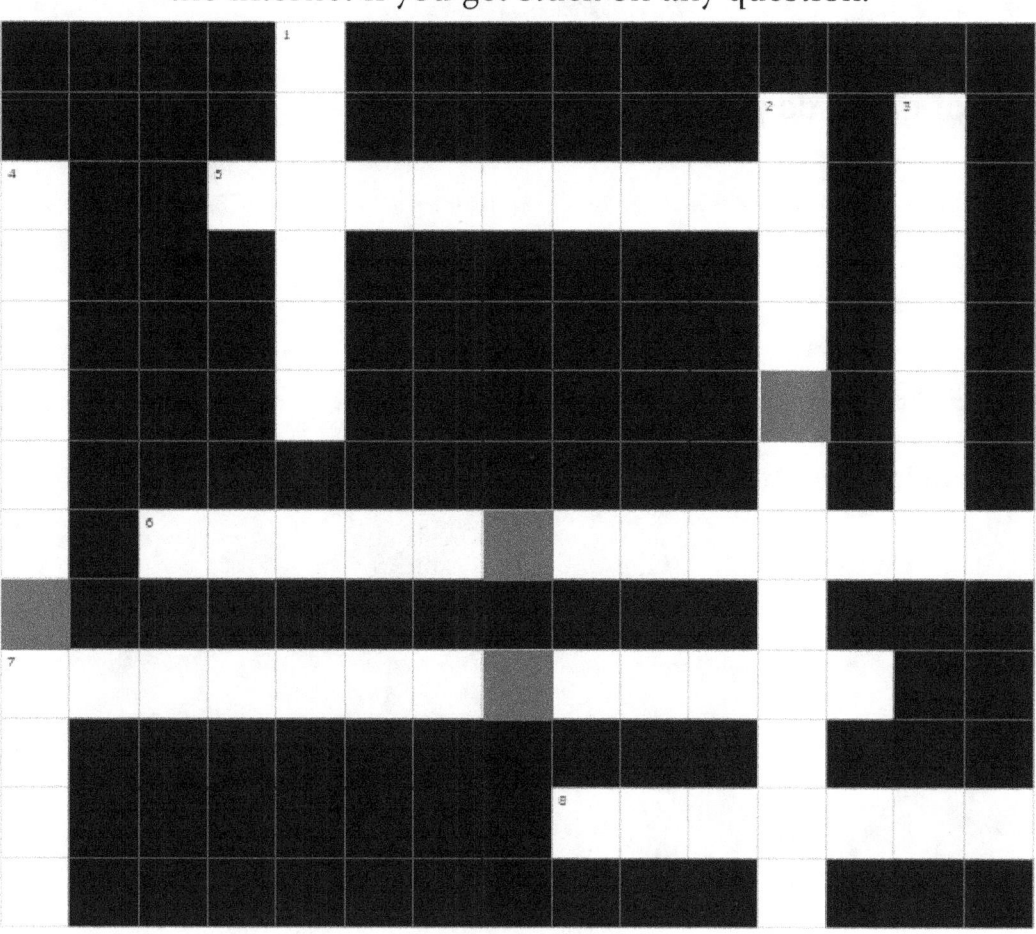

Across
5) Billie was the first black woman to work with a white _____.
6) Billie signed with _____ when she was twenty-nine.
7) Billie's song "_____" was named song of the century by TIME Magazine in 1999.
8) Billie once worked in a _____.

Down
1) Billie toured _____ in 1954 going to Germany, Netherlands, Paris and Switzerland.
2) Billie debuted Strange Fruit in a 1939 performance at _____, New York's first integrated nightclub.
3) "God Bless the Child" was Billie's most popular and most _____ record.
4) Billie made her first appearance on The _____ in 1955, hosted by Steve Allen.

Directions: Read and answer the questions. These are your opinions so the answers will vary.

What kind of music do you like to listen to?

How do musicians create music?

What are some popular musical genres?

Directions: Unscramble the words below about Eleanora. See if you can get the bonus word.

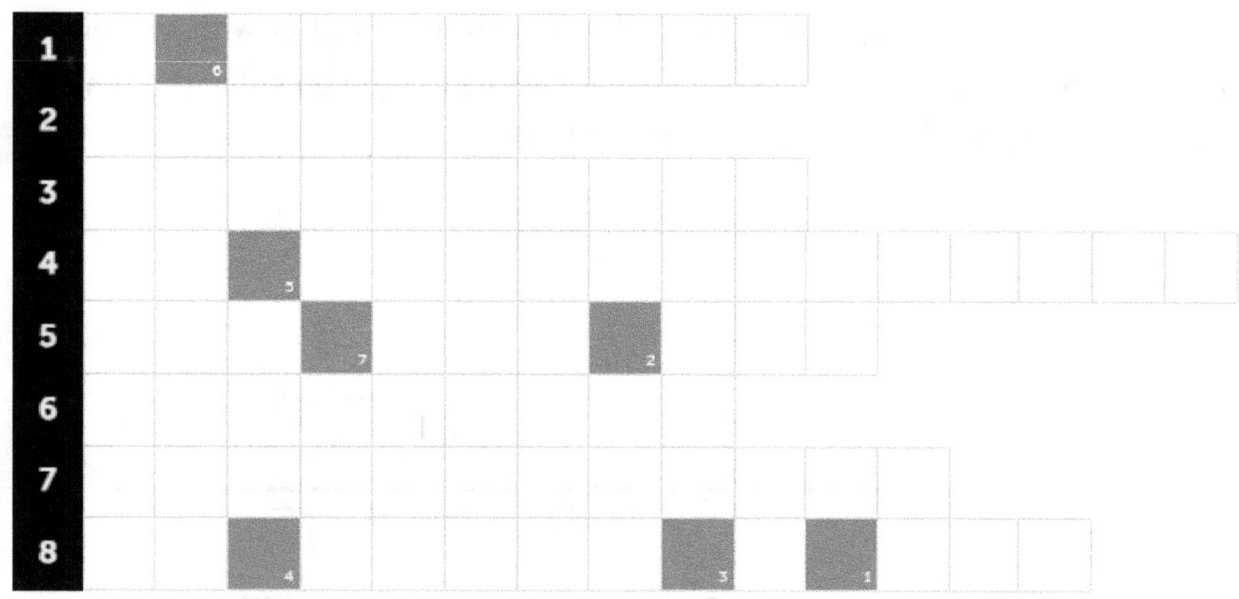

BONUS WORD

| 1 | 2 | 3 | 4 | 5 | 6 | 7 |

Unscramble Words

1) efmalfahol
2) iegnsr
3) giwnsumics
4) odelsdligcebhths
5) anisindytal
6) ssihircro
7) triagestrfun
8) sldnubraeythhm

Directions: This is the WGLT Challenge. Solve the cryptogram. As the puzzle solver, you need to find which number belongs to which character. And this can be pretty challenging! You will need to match the number with the letter. There are some letters given to you below. This will help you solve the other words and unlock more characters. **Good Luck.**

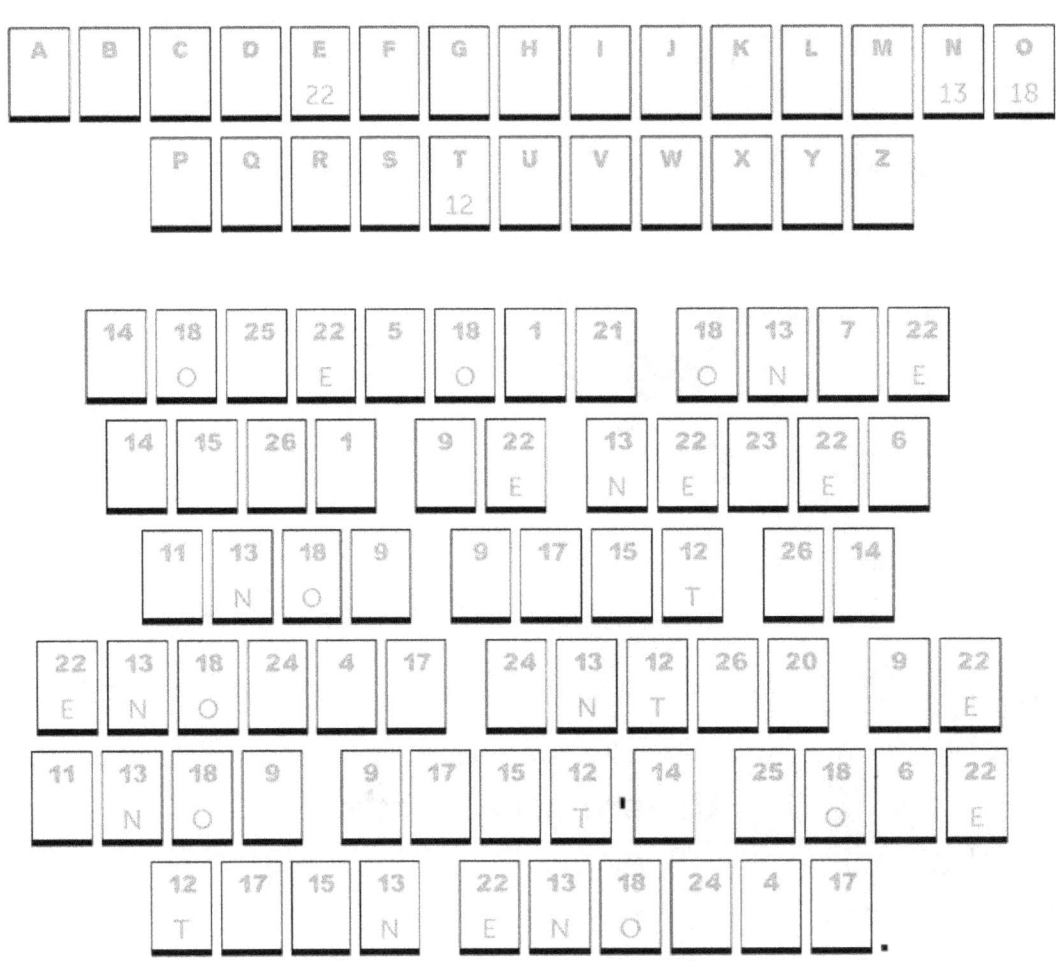

Michael Jackson

August 29, 1958 – June 25, 2009
SINGER / DANCER

43

LEFT BLANK ON PURPOSE

Michael Jackson

Michael Jackson

Michael Jackson

Michael Jackson

Michael Jackson

Michael Jackson

45

Directions: read the bio below and answer the following questions.

Hi, my name is Michael Jackson. I was born on August 29, 1958, in Gary, IN. I was 6 when my dad let me join the family group and our group name was The Jackson 5. In 1967, we won a weekly amateur night concert at the Apollo Theater in Harlem. In 1968, we joined Motown and in 1969, Diana Ross introduced The Jackson 5 to the public. Our first television appearance in 1969 was in the Miss Black America pageant. We performed a cover of "It's Your Thing." From 1972 and 1975, I released four solo studio albums with Motown: Got to Be There (1972), Ben (1972), Music and Me (1973) and Forever, Michael (1975). We signed with Epic Records in 1975 and released six more albums between 1976 and 1984. I released my fifth solo album, Off the Wall, in 1979. In 1982, I released my best-selling and sixth album, Thriller. One of the things I'm best known for is becoming "the King of Pop." Some of the songs I'm known for are "Shake Your Body (Down to the Ground)," "This Place Hotel," and "Can You Feel It."

1. What did the Jackson 5 do at the Apollo Theater?
    A. Win
    B. Lose
    C. Didn't get to perform
2. What year did the Jackson 5 get introduced?
    A. 1968
    B. 1969
    C. 1967
3. Jackson 5 first TV appearance was on what show?
    A. Ed Sullivan Show
    B. American Band Stand
    C. Miss Black America pageant

Directions: Find the words associated with Michael's life and career.

```
D A S P S J D L R O W E H T L A E H
T K F K G A Z J D T K K M L D E M Y
R J S C D C H B A I I N L P F D J O
P Y N D H K U A G H G I J A A V K H
Q C E Z R S C I L W I B T A J I U G
R T Y Y E O L L D L D W E L N Y M W
S J Y Q O N C H U D O D U G W O M U
S R F I G F A E P A Z F O F H F X J
T O Z B O I H X R B J F F V X F N V
K H N Z V V Q M I N P M A A O T S J
L F R G G E C S X O W Y D V M H F S
A C C I W T H L P P I O A L Z E K C
W G F B L R E M V R Z G T N I W V A
N H R M B L I F U C G Q X O D A F C
O U H L M C E T H L W W S I M L E H
O T H V V E I R E R K J R X H L E L
M S U G Q K F J F R V J E N A C I W
Y T E P H I L A N T H R O P I S T D
```

Find These Words

MOTOWNRECORDS OFFTHEWALL SONGWRITER
PHILANTHROPIST KINGOFPOP JACKSONFIVE
THRILLER HALLOFFAME MOONWALK
HEALTHEWORLD

Directions: Read and answer the questions. These are your opinions so the answers will vary.

Can you name some famous musicians from different countries?

How do musicians become successful?

What skills do musicians need to have?

Directions: Read and answer the questions below. There are clues in the puzzle to help you. Try and solve the cryptic message.

Clue for cryptic message: Michael's nickname.

Questions

1) In the West coast of Africa Michael was crowned ____ Sani and given the name Michael Jackson Amalaman Anoh by the tribal chief.

2) Michael has a ____ center named after him in California, "Michael Jackson Burn Center".

3) Michael turned his ranch into a half home half ____ park.

4) Michael is regarded by the RIAA as the ____-selling individual music artist of all time worldwide.

5) Michael loved his llamas and sometimes took them to the ____.

6) Michael invented gravity-____ shoes and had the patent until 2005.

7) Michael ____ on the first-ever Western advertisement commercial in the Soviet Union.

8) Michael was the first artist to have a top-ten single in the ____ Hot 100 in five different decades.

9) Michael had a pet ____ called Bubbles.

Directions: This is the WGLT Challenge. Solve the cryptogram. As the puzzle solver, you need to find which number belongs to which character. And this can be pretty challenging! You will need to match the number with the letter. There are some letters given to you below. This will help you solve the other words and unlock more characters. **Good Luck.**

A	B	C	D	E	F	G	H	I	J	K	L	M	N	O
4			11									1		24

P	Q	R	S	T	U	V	W	X	Y	Z

```
 7  15   '   23  24  7   1   23  16  24
             O       N           O

18  21   4   14  19   5   26  24  14  15  22
          A                    O       M

18  16   4   14  13   1   16   2   7
     T    A             N    T        I

26   7   1   11   7  16   7  16 . 18
 F    I   N   D       T       T     S

 5   7   11  11  21   1   7   1   16   5   21
 H    I    D   D   E   N   I   N    T   H    E

11  14   4   25  21  14   24  26
 D   R    A   W   E   R    O   F

 7   1   1   24  19  21   1  19  21 ,
 I   N   N   O   C   E    N   C   E

25  14   4   20  20  21  11   7   1   4
 W   R    A   P   P   E   D   I   N   A

18  19   4   14  26   24  26   25  24   1   11  21  14 .
 S   C    A   R   F    O   F   W   O    N    D   E   R
```

50

Eunice Kathleen Waymon

Eunice Kathleen Waymon

(February 21, 1933 – April 21, 2003
SINGER

LEFT BLANK ON PURPOSE

Eunice Kathleen Waymon

Eunice Kathleen Waymon

Eunice Kathleen Waymon

Eunice Kathleen Waymon

Eunice Kathleen Waymon

Eunice Kathleen Waymon

Directions: read the bio below and answer the following questions.

Hi, my name is Eunice Waymon. I was born on February 21, 1933, in Tryon, NC. I was around 4 when I learned how to play the piano. I graduated from Allen High School for Girls. I spent some time at Juilliard School in preparation to get into the Curtis Institute of Music but was denied entry, which I think may have happened because of racial prejudice. In 1954, I performed at the Midtown Bar and Grill and changed my stage name to Nina Simone so that my mom wouldn't learn about what I was doing. She felt that the music that I liked was the Devil's music. One of the things I'm best known for is addressing racial inequality in the United States with the song "Mississippi Goddam," which I sang in 1964. This was my response to the June 12, 1963, murder of Medgar Evers and the September 15, 1963, bombing of the 16th Street Baptist Church in Birmingham, Alabama, which killed four young Black girls and partly blinded a fifth. Some of the songs I'm known for are "I Loves You, Porgy," "My Baby Just Cares for Me," "Mississippi Goddam," "Sinnerman," and "Feeling Good."

1. What age did I start playing the piano?
   A. 5
   B. 4
   C. 6
2. What school did I want to get accepted to?
   A. Juilliard School
   B. Curtis Institute of Music
   C. Allen High School for girls
3. I changed my stage name while performing here?
   A. Greenwich Village
   B. Ronnie Scott's Jazz Club
   C. Midtown Bar & Grill

Directions: Answer the questions, to solve the crossword puzzle. You can use the internet if you get stuck on any question.

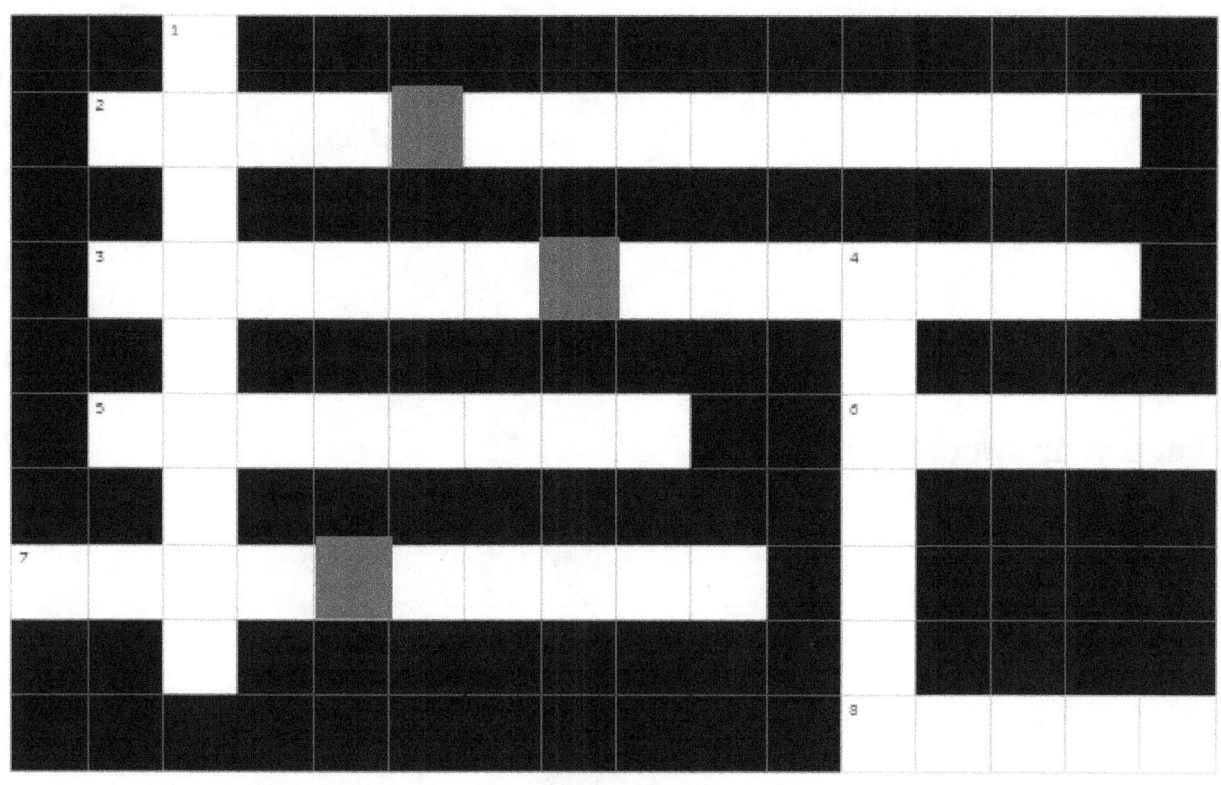

Across

2) Nina's bearing and stage presence earned her the title "the _____ of Soul".

3) Nina wrote "Mississippi Goddam", an outraged response to the murder of Medgar Evers and the Alabama _____ that killed four children in 1963.

5) Nina used her art as a singer, performer and pianist for ____.

6) Nina started playing the ____ by ear at age three.

7) Nina's song "_____" exposed the Eurocentric appearance standards imposed on black women in America

8) Nina believed that shew was a real ____ with a cause.

Down

1) Nina started playing piano at a _____ in Atlantic City.

4) Nina was diagnosed as suffering from ____ disorder.

Directions: Read and answer the questions. These are your opinions so the answers will vary.

How do musicians write lyrics for their songs?

What is your favorite song and why?

Who is your favorite musician and why?

Directions: Unscramble the words below about Eunice. See if you can get the bonus word.

BONUS WORD

Unscramble Words

1) etowrsrnig
2) lrvgiihscit
3) lcalsaics
4) inrges
5) illbteriglutel
6) iatnpsi
7) msairc
8) acootlrtn
9) geospl
10) anteikb

Directions: This is the WGLT Challenge. Solve the cryptogram. As the puzzle solver, you need to find which number belongs to which character. And this can be pretty challenging! You will need to match the number with the letter. There are some letters given to you below. This will help you solve the other words and unlock more characters. **Good Luck.**

June 16, 1971 – September 13, 1996
RAPPER / ACTOR

LEFT BLANK ON PURPOSE

Tupac Amaru Shakur

Tupac Amaru Shakur

Tupac Amaru Shakur

Tupac Amaru Shakur

Tupac Amaru Shakur

Tupac Amaru Shakur

Directions: read the bio below and answer the following questions.

Hi, my name is Lesane Parish Crooks. I was born on June 16, 1971, in New York City, NY. My mom renamed me when I was 1 to Tupac Amaru Shakur. I attended Tamalpais High School in 1988. I did not graduate, but I got my GED later. In 1990, I was a part of the group Digital Underground as a roadie and backup dancer. I debuted in 1991 with the single "Same Song," which was part of the soundtrack for the film Nothing but Trouble. I released my debut album 2Pacalypse Now in 1991. This album addresses social issues that still remain relevant today. In 1993, I released my second album Strictly 4 My N.I.G.G.A.Z. In 1995, while I was locked up, I released what some say is one of the greatest and most influential rap albums: Me Against the World. It debuted as number 1 on the Billboard 200 and sold 240,000 copies in its first week, which set the then-record for the highest first-week sales for a solo male rapper.

1. What did I start my career off doing?
    A. Playing the piano
    B. Backup Dancer
    C. Doing Theater
2. What year did I release arguably my best album?
    A. 1993
    B. 1991
    C. 1995
3. Which song was my come out song in the industry?
    A. Same Song
    B. Dear Mama
    C. Me Against the World

Directions: Find the words associated with Tupac's life and career.

D	I	G	I	T	A	L	U	N	D	E	R	G	R	O	U	N	D
T	D	E	A	T	H	R	O	W	R	E	C	O	R	D	S	F	W
H	Y	R	M	I	R	E	H	T	E	V	O	B	A	U	T	K	Y
U	M	C	L	I	N	S	N	W	S	L	R	O	Z	I	J	X	I
G	E	N	E	S	R	Q	C	U	D	P	F	K	K	P	T	R	A
L	B	G	P	B	Z	Y	V	P	A	X	U	U	I	Z	D	Q	U
I	K	K	U	F	D	L	J	O	I	H	I	G	H	D	D	B	N
F	H	L	O	D	A	D	I	E	L	G	H	A	X	A	F	M	A
E	P	B	G	I	L	V	L	T	J	I	L	Q	S	K	B	W	C
X	H	C	Q	C	X	I	B	R	H	L	K	G	I	F	T	K	U
E	P	S	F	Y	D	G	L	Y	O	K	E	Q	W	R	R	A	I
N	B	X	R	W	E	B	E	F	U	K	Q	G	X	A	A	P	P
N	D	S	B	E	A	H	F	T	I	L	S	Z	P	C	X	E	U
B	L	A	C	K	P	A	N	T	H	E	R	P	A	R	T	Y	N
V	W	O	Z	N	M	X	K	J	L	E	E	N	P	A	B	P	V
M	G	C	J	E	I	U	A	H	V	R	W	B	V	B	X	W	T
Q	R	E	C	I	T	S	U	J	C	I	T	E	O	P	Z	U	B
B	A	C	K	U	P	D	A	N	C	E	R	S	R	V	L	X	I

Find These Words

BLACKPANTHERPARTY RAPPER ABOVETHERIM
HALLOFFAME POETRY DIGITALUNDERGROUND
BACKUPDANCER THUGLIFE POETICJUSTICE
DEATHROWRECORDS

Directions: Read and answer the questions. These are your opinions so the answers will vary.

What kind of instruments do musicians play?

What is your favorite genre of music and why?

What is the difference between a singer and a musician?

Directions: Read and answer the questions below. There are clues in the puzzle to help you. Try and solve the cryptic message.

Clue for cryptic message: This is one of Tupac's albums.

Questions

1) Tupac studied at the _____ School of Performing Arts.
2) Tupac's parents were black _____ members.
3) Tupac started his entertainment career as a ____ dancer for The Digital Underground.
4) Tupac's first film _____ was in the 1991 film Nothing but Trouble.
5) Tupac was signed to Interscope Records by Tom Whalley (who still _____ his estate today),
6) Tupac's fourth album, "All Eyez on Me," was a certified _____ platinum.
7) Tupac played Travis Younger in A Raisin in the Sun, at the ____ Theater in Harlem, NY.
8) Tupac last name "Shakur" comes from _____ origins and means "thankful" or "appreciative."

65

Directions: This is the WGLT Challenge. Solve the cryptogram. As the puzzle solver, you need to find which number belongs to which character. And this can be pretty challenging! You will need to match the number with the letter. There are some letters given to you below. This will help you solve the other words and unlock more characters. **Good Luck.**

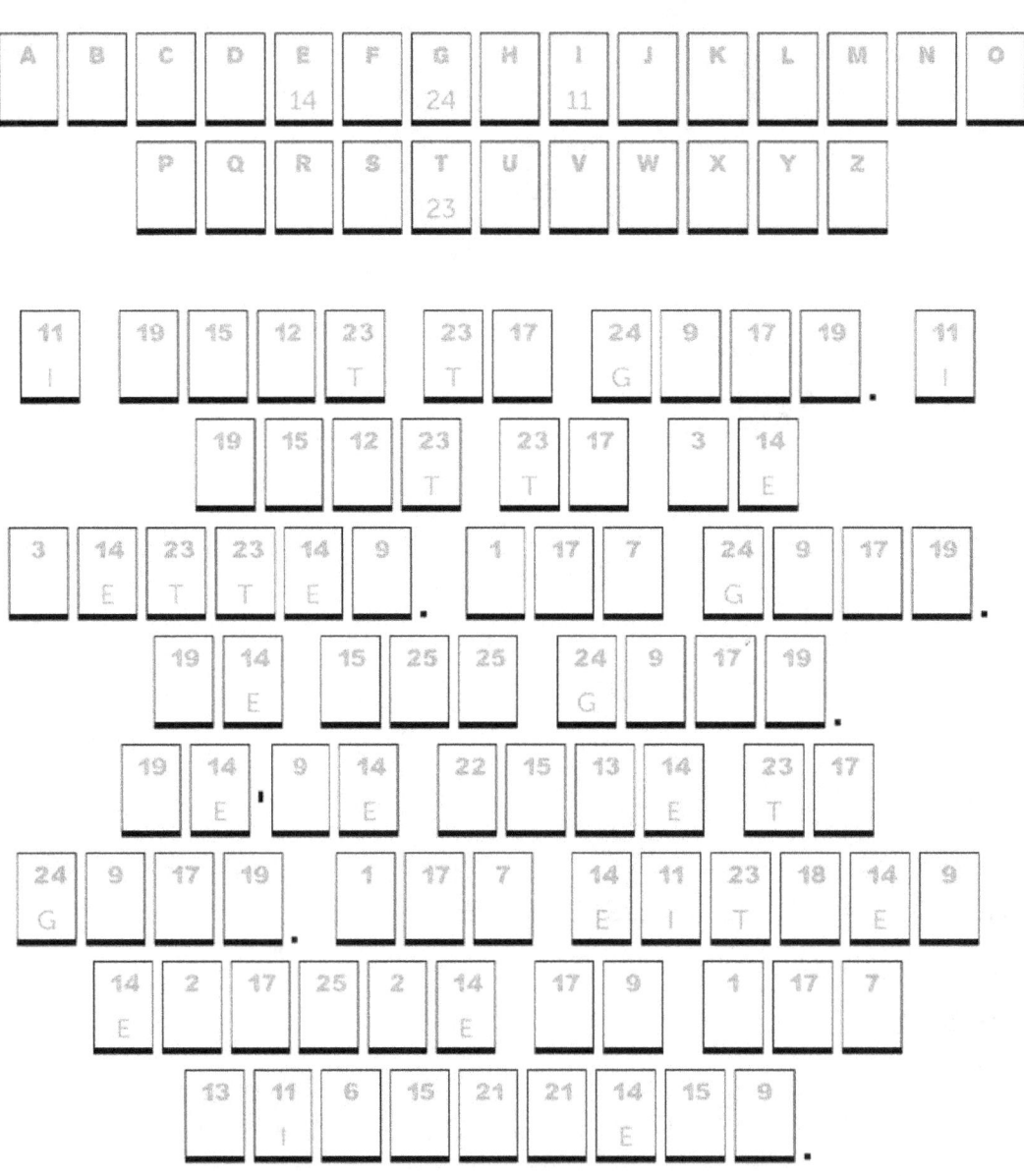

Whitney Houston

Whitney Houston

August 9, 1963 – February 11, 2012
SINGER

LEFT BLANK ON PURPOSE

Whitney Houston

Whitney Houston

Whitney Houston

Whitney Houston

Whitney Houston

Whitney Houston

Directions: read the bio below and answer the following questions.

Hi, my name is **Whitney Houston**. I was born on August 9, 1963, in Newark, NJ. In 1981, I graduated from Mount Saint Dominic Academy. My first hit was a duet with Teddy Pendergrass in 1984, which was called "Hold Me." It was a top 5 RGB hit. I released my debut album Whitney Houston in 1985. It was the best-selling debut album by a solo artist. I released my second album, Whitney, in 1987. My second album was more successful than my first one. I set a record total of seven consecutive number-one hits. I became the first woman to generate four number-one singles from one album. The album Whitney was given a Diamond certification in the US. In 1992, I had my first acting role as the star of the film The Bodyguard. The movie's soundtrack lead single was "I Will Always Love You." It was my first Diamond single; it sold 20 million copies and became the best-selling single by a female solo artist of all time. One of the things I'm best known for is, according to Guinness World Records, being the most-awarded female act of all time.

1. What was my first hit song?
   A. You Give Good Love
   B. Hold Me
   C. I Will Always Love You
2. I set a record with how many consecutive #1 hits?
   A. 8
   B. 6
   C. 7
3. I have a Guinness World Record for what?
   A. Most Diamond Singles
   B. Most awarded female act
   C. Most singles sold

Directions: Answer the questions, to solve the crossword puzzle. You can use the internet if you get stuck on any question.

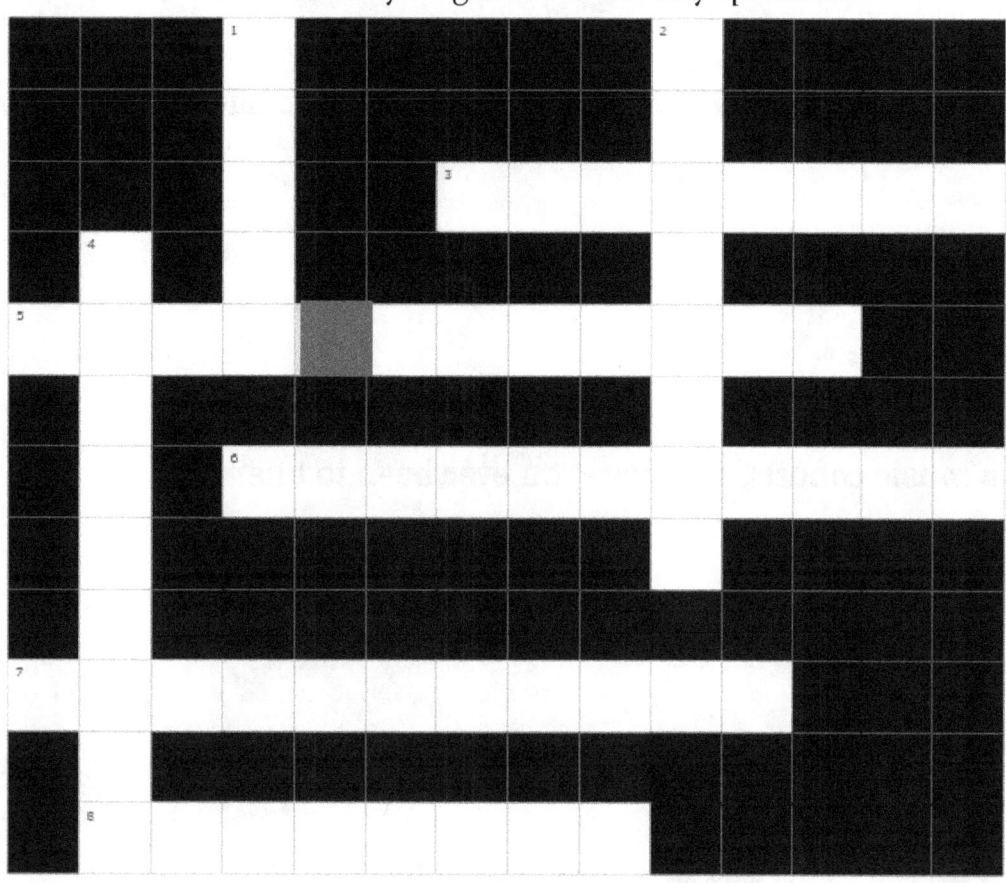

Across

3) Whitney's debut self-titled album has been listed as one of the 500 _____ Albums of All Time by Rolling Stone.

5) Whitney's song "I Will Always Love You" became the _____ physical single by a woman in music history.

6) Whitney is the only artist to have had seven _____ number-one singles on the Billboard Hot 100.

7) Whitney's first recorded duet was with Teddy _____, "Hold Me".

8) Whitney's management company, Nippy Inc., was named after her childhood ___.

Down

1) Whitney's hit cover of "I Will Always Love You" is the number _____ best-selling song of all time, having sold over 24 million copies.

2) All of Whitney's albums have all gone _____ or gold certified.

4) Whitney was one of the first black women to appear on the cover of___.

Directions: Read and answer the questions. These are your opinions so the answers will vary.

What is a famous song that you like, and who is the musician that performed it?

What is a music concert, and have you ever been to one?

What is a music video, and have you ever watched one?

Directions: Unscramble the words below about Whitney. See if you can get the bonus word.

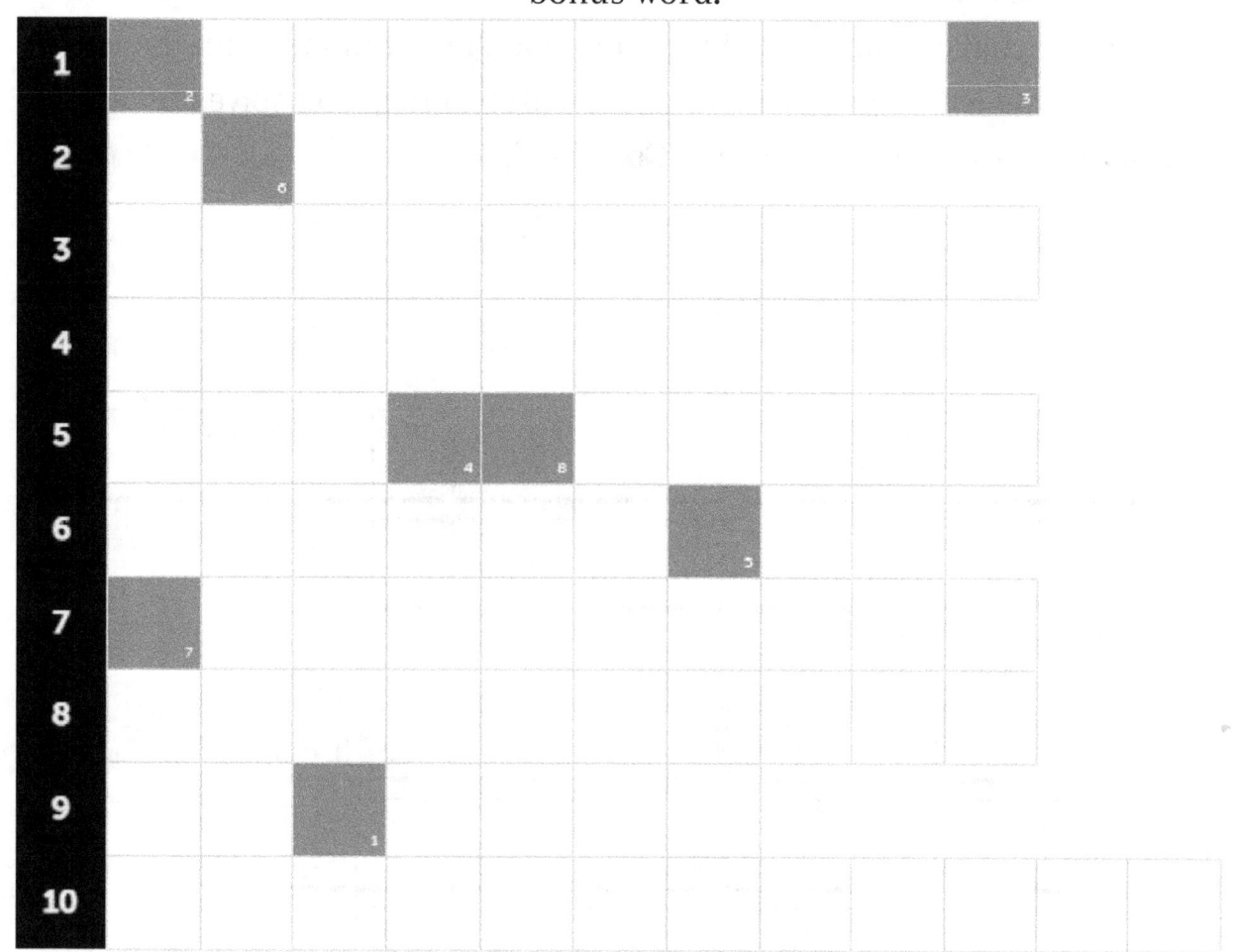

BONUS WORD

Unscramble Words

1) lmahoalfef
2) inserg
3) damwysaemr
4) dayudgobr
5) livivcsaed
6) vrulswpeob
7) lailrncede
8) nwrobybobb
9) arcsest
10) rgsamwmryaad

73

Directions: This is the WGLT Challenge. Solve the cryptogram. As the puzzle solver, you need to find which number belongs to which character. And this can be pretty challenging! You will need to match the number with the letter. There are some letters given to you below. This will help you solve the other words and unlock more characters. **Good Luck.**

O'Shea Jackson Sr.

O'Shea Jackson Sr.

June 15, 1969 - PRESENT
RAPPER / FILMMAKER

LEFT BLANK ON PURPOSE

O'Shea Jackson Sr.

O'Shea Jackson Sr.

O'Shea Jackson Sr.

O'Shea Jackson Sr.

O'Shea Jackson Sr.

O'Shea Jackson Sr.

Directions: read the bio below and answer the following questions.

Hi, my name is O'Shea Jackson Sr. I was born on June 15, 1969, in Los Angeles, CA. I got a degree in architectural drafting from Phoenix Institute of Technology in 1988 as a backup plan. I was 16 when I sold my first song "Boyz- n-the-Hood" to Eazy-E. I was a part of N.W.A until 1989, which is when Jerry Heller started messing with my compensation. I started my solo career and released my debut album AmeriKKKa's Most Wanted in 1990. Later that year, I released the EP Kill At Will. It was the first rap EP that received a Platinum certification. In 1991, I released my second album, Death Certificate, which had the track "No Vaseline." This song responded to the dis from N.W.A's dis track. In 1992, I released my third album, The Predator. This album was the first album ever to debut at No. 1 on both the RGB/hip-hop and pop charts. Some of the movies that I've starred in are Boyz n the Hood, Trespass, Next Friday, Friday After Next, Barbershop and XXX.

1. How old was I when I sold my first song?
   A. 21
   B. 16
   C. 14
2. What album was rap's first EP certified Platinum?
   A. Kill At Will
   B. AmeriKKKA's Most Wanted
   C. Predator
3. What is my degree in?
   A. Computers
   B. Education
   C. Architectural Drafting

Directions: Find the words associated with O'Shea's life and career.

Q	Z	N	E	X	S	E	L	E	G	N	A	S	O	L	A	X	G
D	L	M	T	M	F	C	W	Z	F	V	R	B	F	K	T	A	V
Q	R	I	D	E	A	L	O	N	G	Z	M	Z	I	J	N	M	G
Y	E	H	Y	V	A	Y	T	C	D	G	F	I	F	G	Y	R	O
S	M	C	N	P	I	Q	P	L	U	S	Q	B	S	K	N	F	E
E	A	O	L	N	G	I	B	N	B	B	F	T	Z	X	I	D	O
J	F	S	B	M	N	C	X	N	Q	V	E	O	H	V	B	F	T
P	F	C	A	J	A	E	U	E	J	R	F	R	D	K	O	H	M
R	O	V	I	W	X	E	G	B	R	I	E	P	N	I	U	T	R
H	L	R	E	P	P	A	R	A	E	K	N	O	Z	R	A	U	F
A	L	L	M	M	G	D	P	V	A	V	D	L	B	F	N	Y	I
Q	A	.	H	E	S	Q	C	M	F	F	I	H	G	M	I	Y	N
U	H	A	R	A	L	V	M	B	A	B	U	S	O	D	G	K	S
C	S	.	K	Q	C	L	V	J	O	H	G	Q	I	W	Q	C	J
M	J	W	U	W	I	P	L	J	G	A	E	C	T	O	E	C	W
Z	U	.	G	F	X	T	E	N	J	N	D	J	Q	N	N	W	W
S	P	N	Y	A	D	I	R	F	T	X	E	N	W	S	O	W	J
K	O	B	C	P	O	H	S	R	E	B	R	A	B	W	Y	B	T

Find These Words

RAPPER NEXTFRIDAY FILMMAKER
GANGSTERRAP RIDEALONG CUBEVISION
HALLOFFAME N.W.A. LOSANGELES
BARBERSHOP

Directions: Read and answer the questions. These are your opinions so the answers will vary.

How do musicians write their songs, and what tools do they use?

What is your favorite musical instrument, and have you ever played one?

Who is the most famous musician in the world, and what do you know about them?

Directions: Read and answer the questions below. There are clues in the puzzle to help you. Try and solve the cryptic message.

Clue for cryptic message: One of O'Shea's 40 plus movies he's been in.

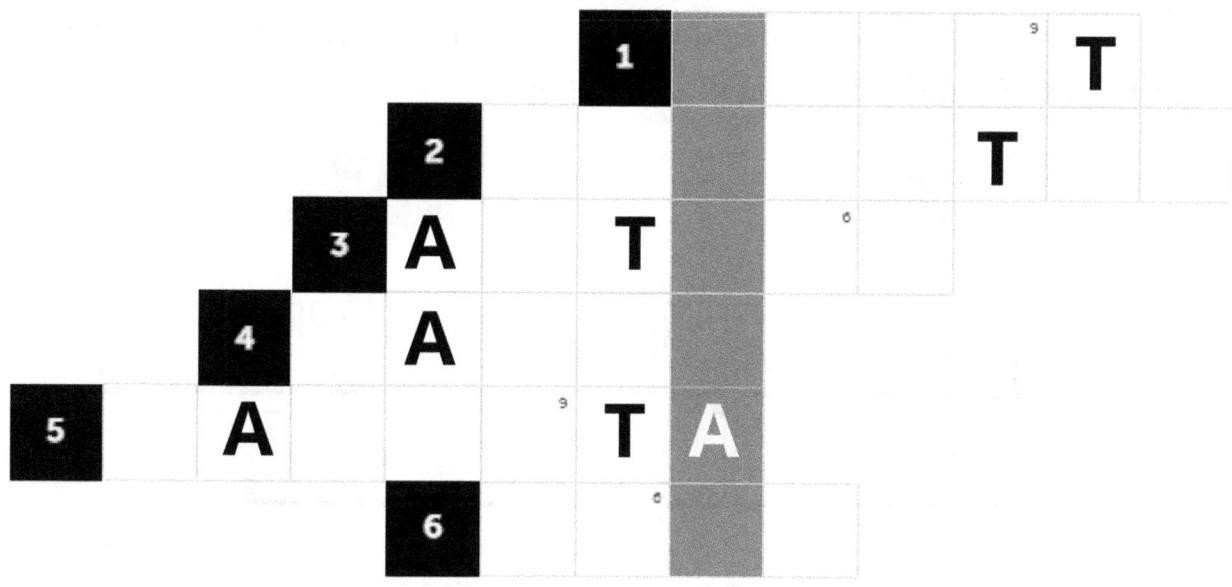

Questions

1) O'Shea's EP: Kill At Will was the ____ hip hop EP to of ever go Platinum.
2) O'Shea's movie The Players Club is the first film where he was the ____, producer, writer and actor.
3) O'Shea was in the group Cru' in ____ before he joined N.W.A.
4) O'Shea's clothing line is ____ Solo.
5) O'Shea helped formed the ____ rap group N.W.A.
6) O'Shea started in the movie ___ n the Hood as the character Doughboy.

Directions: This is the WGLT Challenge. Solve the cryptogram. As the puzzle solver, you need to find which number belongs to which character. And this can be pretty challenging! You will need to match the number with the letter. There are some letters given to you below. This will help you solve the other words and unlock more characters. **Good Luck.**

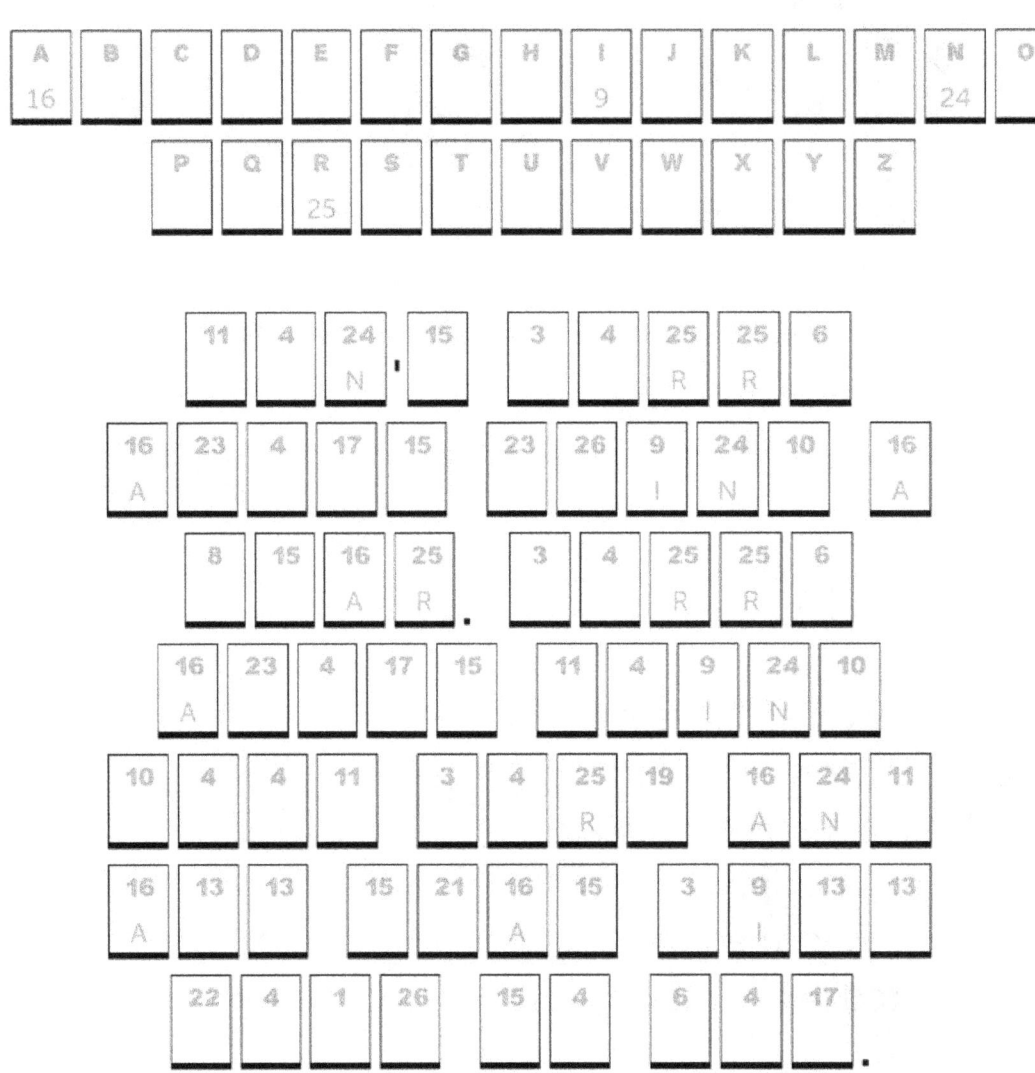

A	B	C	D	E	F	G	H	I	J	K	L	M	N	O
16								9					24	

P	Q	R	S	T	U	V	W	X	Y	Z
		25								

11 4 24 15 · 3 4 25 25 6
       N   R R

16 23 4 17 15 23 26 9 24 10 16
A   I   N   A

8 15 16 25 . 3 4 25 25 6
      A   R   R R

16 23 4 17 15 11 4 9 24 10
A   I   N

10 4 4 11 3 4 25 19 16 24 11
                        R   A   N

16 13 13 15 21 16 15 3 9 13 13
A   A   I

22 4 1 26 15 4 6 4 17 .

Ella Fitzgerald

Ella Fitzgerald

April 25, 1917 – June 15, 1996
JAZZ SINGER

83

LEFT BLANK ON PURPOSE

Ella Fitzgerald

Ella Fitzgerald

Ella Fitzgerald

Ella Fitzgerald

Ella Fitzgerald

Ella Fitzgerald

Directions: read the bio below and answer the following questions.

Hi, my name is Ella Fitzgerald. I was born on April 25, 1917, in Newport News, VA. When I was 17, I performed at Amateur Nights at the Apollo Theater. I sang "Judy" and "The Object of My Affection" and won first prize. After that, I started singing with Chick Webb's orchestra until he died in 1939. I took the role of bandleader and we renamed the band to Ella and Her Famous Orchestra. In 1938, I co-wrote a rendition of the nursery rhyme "A-Tisket, ATasket," which was probably my biggest record. It was a huge hit on the radio. I recorded nearly 150 songs with Webb's orchestra between 1935 and 1942 and gained the nickname "The First Lady of Song." In 1958, I became the first African American woman to win a Grammy Award. I was also the first Black woman to headline at the famous Copacabana nightclub. I gave my final performance at New York City's famed Carnegie Hall. It was my 26th time performing there. One of the things that I'm best known for is defining different styles, such as swing and bebop.

1. What got me started in my singing career?
    A. I was notice in a Night Club
    B. Winning Amateur Nights at the Apollo Theater
    C. My Church
2. What was my biggest song?
    A. A-Tisket, A-Tasket
    B. Love and Kisses
    C. It Don't Mean a Thing (If It Ain't Got That Swing)
3. I was the first African American woman to?
    A. Have a Platinum song
    B. Perform at the Super Bowl
    C. Win a Grammy Award

Directions: Answer the questions, to solve the crossword puzzle. You can use the internet if you get stuck on any question.

Across

5) Ella made her film debut in 1942's Ride 'Em Cowboy, with _____ and Costello movie.

8) Ella performed at _____ twenty-six times including her last performance.

Down

1) Ella along with Carol Channing, became the first celebrity singer at the _____.

2) Ella started out as a _____ at the Apollo Theater.

3) Marilyn Monroe helped Ella to get booked at popular '50s nightclub _____.

4) The Ella Fitzgerald Charitable Foundation, provides aid to _____ and families by fostering a love for music and reading.

6) Ella won a total of _____ GRAMMYs.

7) Ella's revamped song "A-Tisket, A-Tasket" is still a _____ standard.

Directions: Read and answer the questions. These are your opinions so the answers will vary.

Who is your favorite musician or band, and why do you like their music?

_____

_____

What instruments do musicians typically use to make music?

_____

_____

How do musicians write songs?

_____

_____

_____

_____

Directions: Unscramble the words below about Ella. See if you can get the bonus word.

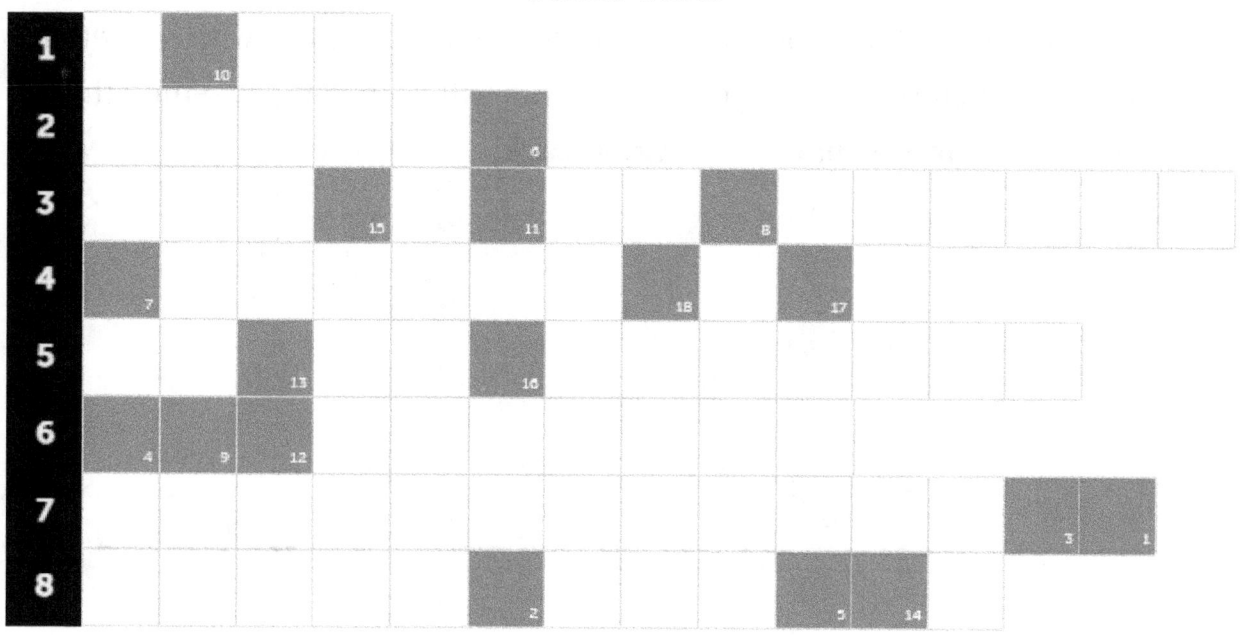

BONUS WORD

Unscramble Words

1) zzaj
2) grinse
3) rsadsweaperntid
4) inaisgsgcnt
5) eploahertlato
6) mhonlgfyei
7) sekaatttaektis
8) fhteaeiknmkc

Directions: This is the WGLT Challenge. Solve the cryptogram. As the puzzle solver, you need to find which number belongs to which character. And this can be pretty challenging! You will need to match the number with the letter. There are some letters given to you below. This will help you solve the other words and unlock more characters. **Good Luck.**

Miles Dewey Davis III

May 26, 1926 – September 28, 1991
TRUMPETER / COMPOSER

LEFT BLANK ON PURPOSE

Miles Dewey Davis III

Miles Dewey Davis III

Miles Dewey Davis III

Miles Dewey Davis III

Miles Dewey Davis III

Miles Dewey Davis III

Directions: read the bio below and answer the following questions.

Hi, my name is Miles Dewey Davis III. I was born on May 26, 1926, in Alton, IL. I graduated from East St. Louis Lincoln High School in 1944. Later that year, I auditioned for the Institute of Musical Arts, which later became known as the Juilliard School, in New York City and I was accepted. I took classes in music theory, piano and dictation. Shortly after my third semester, I dropped out to focus on my music full-time. In 1948, I declined an offer to join Duke Ellington's orchestra so that I could focus on my project Birth of the Cool. I also didn't want to play the same music night after night. Between 1948 and 1957, I played with several artists and bands. We released many singles that were compiled in 1957 for my album Birth of the Cool, which brought a new form of jazz, into the light, which was famously known as cool jazz. Some of the songs I'm known for are "I Fall in Love Too Easily," "Round About Midnight," "Some Day My Prince Will Come," "If I Were a Bell," and "My Funny Valentine."

1. What school did I go to for music theory?
   A. Juilliard School
   B. East St. Louis Lincoln High School
   C. Manhattan School of Music
2. What year did Cool Jazz begin?
   A. 1948
   B. 1957
   C. 1953
3. I dropped out of Institute of Musical Arts to focus on?
   A. Music
   B. Dancing
   C. Theater

Directions: Find the words associated with Miles's life and career.

```
P H K Z O G D L Q J A Z Z K V V O O
U D X B W S W U T X G E H C R O R N
X G L H A R D B O P O A A W Z X J I
U W C E B N H G N R T K L M K M A E
B X T T S A I J P Y L N L A M W F B
J P M R L D N O L B F H O W X T R Z
O J Z U X I R D R C L E F A S J I Y
U I V S S L U L L E I U F H U E C O
N A N C A I T N J E H X A K K J A A
O W Y C B R C W W I A B M M M A N P
P K R R Q Y T I Y U F D E R S Z R W
K Y R P U E N S A M N F E C V V H R
S J G I I S C O E N M S P R S S Y D
W H Q U N Z R D O H G F K Q Z N T B
Z B X K T D G W K Q C I G F C J H O
H C D J E Q I P D R N R C G O T M D
A I X Q T D F T O A E K O S W K S C
G T B P M E F E F R E T E P M U R T
```

Find These Words

HARDBOP QUINTET HEROIN
TRUMPETER BANDLEADER HALLOFFAME
JAZZ AFRICANRHYTHMS MUSICIAN
ORCHESTRAS

Directions: Read and answer the questions. These are your opinions so the answers will vary.

Can you name some famous musicians from different parts of the world?

What is a concert, and what happens at one?

How do musicians prepare for a live performance?

Directions: Read and answer the questions below. There are clues in the puzzle to help you. Try and solve the cryptic message.

Clue for cryptic message: One of Miles's many talents.

Questions

1) Miles was inducted at ____ and Roll Hall of Fame.
2) Miles _____ out of Juilliard School of Music because he wanted to perform full-time.
3) Miles used a ____ on his trumpet.
4) Miles received his first _____ as a gift from John Eubanks, a friend of his father.
5) Miles was known as the father of ____ Jazz.
6) Miles's album 'Kind of Blues", is regarded as the ____ jazz album of all time.
7) Miles formed the first ____ the Miles Davis Quintet for a performance at Café Bohemia.
8) Miles was _____ to Cicely Tyson.

97

Directions: This is the WGLT Challenge. Solve the cryptogram. As the puzzle solver, you need to find which number belongs to which character. And this can be pretty challenging! You will need to match the number with the letter. There are some letters given to you below. This will help you solve the other words and unlock more characters. **Good Luck.**

Diana Ross

Diana Ross

March 26, 1944 - PRESENT
ENTERTAINER / ACTRESS

99

LEFT BLANK ON PURPOSE

Diana Ross

Diana Ross

Diana Ross

Diana Ross

Diana Ross

Diana Ross

Directions: read the bio below and answer the following questions.

Hi, my name is Diana Ross. I was born on March 26, 1944, in Detroit, MI. In 1962, I graduated from Cass Technical High School, which was a four-year college and preparatory magnet school. When I was 15, I joined the Primettes. We won a talent competition in 1960 and were invited to audition for Motown Records. However, we weren't signed until 1961. At this time, we changed our name to The Supremes. We released our first hit song, which was "When the Lovelight Starts Shining Through His Eyes," and it peaked at 23 on the Billboard Hot 100. We never looked back. We dominated the 60s with multiple number-one hits. I went solo in 1970 when I released my debut album, Diana Ross. My single "I'm Still Waiting" was my first number-one single in the UK. In 1972, I starred in my first film, Lady Sings the Blues. One of the things I'm best known for is being the first African American woman to co-host the Academy Awards.

1. What got me an audition with Motown Records?
    A. A&R Rep
    B. Won talent contest
    C. Family
2. What year did I start my solo career?
    A. 1960
    B. 1972
    C. 1970
3. I was the first African American woman to what?
    A. Go Diamond
    B. Co-host the Academy Awards
    C. Co-host the NAACP Awards

Directions: Answer the questions, to solve the crossword puzzle. You can use the internet if you get stuck on any question.

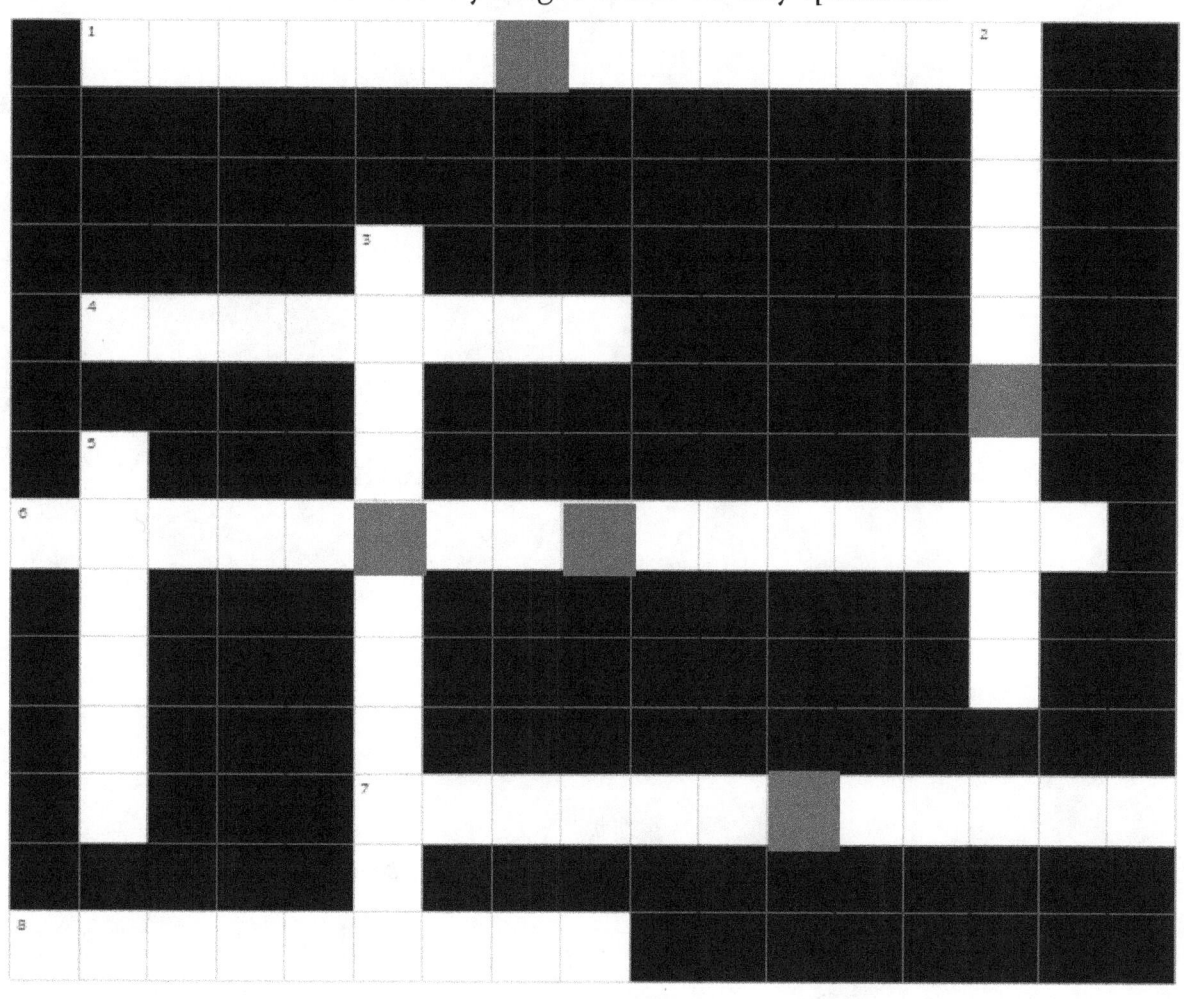

Across

1) Diana worked as a secretary for _____ before she was signed as an artist.
4) Diana was inducted to the Rock and Roll Hall of Fame as a member of the _____.
6) Diana was awarded the Presidential _____.
7) Diana has never won a _____ for her music.
8) Diana likes to support _____ charities.

Down

2) Diana performed in the half-time show at _____ XXX.
3) Diana was the _____ of the vocal group the Supremes.
5) Diana is the most successful _____ artist of all time, with over 70 hit singles to her name.

Directions: Read and answer the questions. These are your opinions so the answers will vary.

What are some different genres of music, and can you name some musicians who play in those genres?

What is a music video, and how do musicians make them?

What is the difference between a solo artist and a band?

Directions: Unscramble the words below about Diana. See if you can get the bonus word.

BONUS WORD

Unscramble Words

1) srseethemup
2) tmoown
3) ewziht
4) alflaohemf
5) elhdlbilaoiyi
6) rdgaieesnl
7) nagchimi
8) noagmhay
9) boeblyva

Directions: This is the WGLT Challenge. Solve the cryptogram. As the puzzle solver, you need to find which number belongs to which character. And this can be pretty challenging! You will need to match the number with the letter. There are some letters given to you below. This will help you solve the other words and unlock more characters. **Good Luck.**

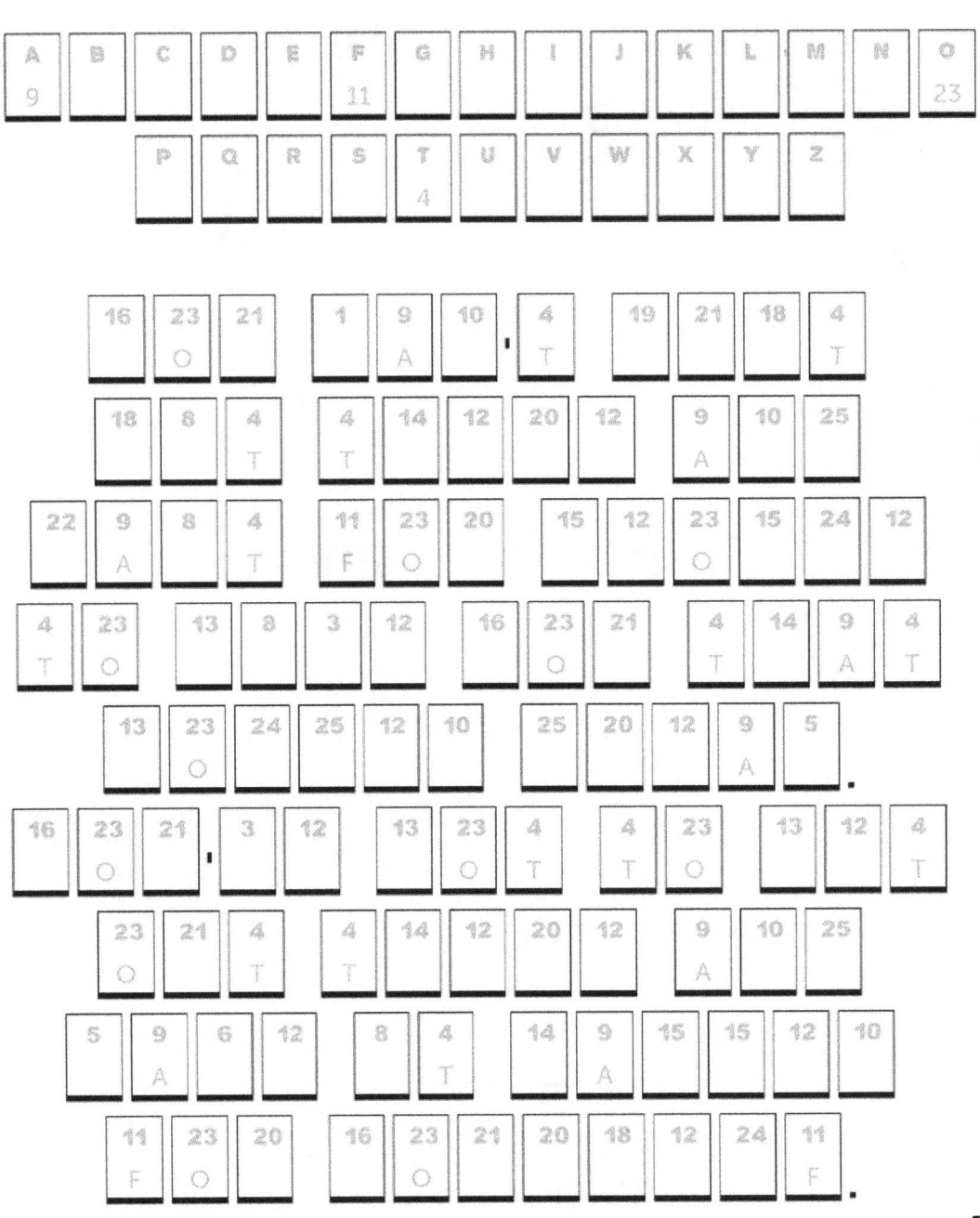

106

December 4, 1969 - PRESENT
RAPPER

LEFT BLANK ON PURPOSE

Shawn Carter

Shawn Carter

Shawn Carter

Shawn Carter

Shawn Carter

Shawn Carter

Directions: read the bio below and answer the following questions.

Hi, my name is Shawn Carter. I was born on December 4, 1969, in Brooklyn, NY. I attended George Westinghouse Career and Technical Education High School with rappers The Notorious B.I.G. and Busta Rhymes and later attended Trenton Central High School. I was known around Brooklyn, but no major label would give me a record deal. In 1995, I started my own label, Roc-A-Fella Records and we got a distribution deal from Priority Records. I release my debut album in 1996, which was called Reasonable Doubt. It reached 23 on the Billboard 200. We reached a new distribution deal with Def Jam Records in 1997 and I released my next album, In My Lifetime, Vol 1. I was the first rapper to be honored in the Songwriters Hall of Fame. I was the first solo living rapper to be inducted into the Rock and Roll Hall of Fame. Some of the albums I'm known for are The Blueprint (2001), The Black Album (2003), American Gangster (2007) and 4:44 (2017) to name a few.

1. Who didn't I go to High School with?
    A. Kanye West
    B. Notorious B.I.G.
    C. Busta Rhymes
2. What year did I help found Roc-A-Fella Records?
    A. 1999
    B. 1996
    C. 1995
3. I was the first solo rapper to do what?
    A. Go Diamond
    B. Be a millionaire
    C. Be inducted in the Rock and Roll Hall of Fame

Directions: Find the words associated with Shawn's life and career.

D	N	C	L	J	M	U	B	L	A	K	C	A	L	B	E	H	T
M	V	B	W	S	D	R	A	W	A	Y	M	M	A	R	G	E	Q
I	M	G	N	Q	Z	X	C	O	G	T	J	P	R	V	L	U	D
U	O	R	B	O	D	I	M	V	H	R	V	E	E	T	P	R	L
B	N	D	A	J	Q	Z	B	S	C	O	C	N	Z	L	W	T	Q
D	O	N	R	G	J	J	D	Q	S	U	T	W	K	C	U	Z	B
V	G	R	I	V	G	M	X	S	D	R	O	B	T	J	O	F	W
N	R	O	A	W	N	V	W	O	E	T	M	Q	D	Z	R	U	J
O	A	W	A	P	C	U	R	P	D	P	T	P	V	S	U	T	F
I	M	F	D	S	P	P	R	A	W	E	U	V	N	G	P	U	M
T	U	I	P	W	D	E	Y	I	F	J	O	Q	W	A	Q	T	Y
A	T	S	M	R	N	F	R	T	W	R	R	A	N	G	L	F	E
N	E	E	O	E	H	A	L	L	O	F	F	A	M	E	Z	R	H
C	F	C	U	K	G	X	A	U	Q	O	Q	L	M	T	F	P	R
O	E	R	D	F	Q	B	I	L	L	I	O	N	A	I	R	E	B
R	M	M	Z	K	U	B	L	P	Q	U	P	M	U	L	S	G	E
R	O	C	-	A	-	F	E	L	L	A	R	E	C	O	R	D	S
Q	N	R	Y	C	A	X	T	C	Z	M	H	K	D	I	U	D	Z

Find These Words

HALLOFFAME ENTREPRENEUR RAPPER
THEBLACKALBUM MONOGRAM ROCNATION
BILLIONAIRE RECORDPRODUCER GRAMMYAWARDS
ROC-A-FELLARECORDS

Directions: Read and answer the questions. These are your opinions so the answers will vary.

How has music changed over time, and what are some examples of different eras in music history?

_____

_____

Who is your favorite musician, and why do you like their music?

_____

_____

Can you name some instruments that musicians play, and what type of music they are used for?

_____

_____

_____

_____

_____

Directions: Read and answer the questions below. There are clues in the puzzle to help you. Try and solve the cryptic message.

Clue for cryptic message: One of Shawn's investments.

Questions

1) Shawn co-owns the 40/40 Club in _____ City.
2) Shawn lived in _____ during the late 1980's.
3) Shawn founded the sports agency _____ Sports.
4) Shawn was president of _____ records.
5) Shawn was the first rapper to be inducted into the _____ Hall of Fame.
6) Shawn was the first solo living _____ inducted in the Rock and Roll Hall of Fame.
7) Michael _____ sang the background vocals on Shawn's single "Girls, Girls, Girls".
8) "Hard Knock Life" was Shawn's most _____ successful album.

Directions: This is the WGLT Challenge. Solve the cryptogram. As the puzzle solver, you need to find which number belongs to which character. And this can be pretty challenging! You will need to match the number with the letter. There are some letters given to you below. This will help you solve the other words and unlock more characters. **Good Luck.**

Hazel Scott

Hazel Scott

115

June 11, 1920 – October 2, 1981
JAZZ AND CLASSICAL PIANIST

LEFT BLANK ON PURPOSE

Hazel Scott

Hazel Scott

Hazel Scott

Hazel Scott

Hazel Scott

Hazel Scott

Directions: read the bio below and answer the following questions.

Hi, my name is Hazel Scott. I was born on June 11, 1920, in Port of Spain, Trinidad and Tobago. My mom was a classically trained pianist and music teacher. By the time I turned 4, I could play anything I heard on the piano. I was labeled as a child prodigy and was accepted into the Juilliard School of Music. By 16, I regularly performed in radio programs for the Mutual Broadcasting System. I performed jazz, blues, ballads, Broadway and boogie-woogie songs and classical music at various nightclubs. I was featured in Café Society's "From Bach to Boogie-Woogie" concerts in 1941 and 1943 at Carnegie Hall. I was one of the first Black women to gain respectable roles in major Hollywood pictures, such as Broadway Rhythm (MGM, 1944) with Lena Horne and The Heat's On (Columbia, 1943). One of the things I'm best known for is becoming the first African American to have my own TV show in America, The Hazel Scott Show, which was released in 1950.

1. What music instrument was I able to play by age four?
   A. Trumpet
   B. Piano
   C. Guitar
2. How old was I when I started performing radio?
   A. 18
   B. 14
   C. 16
3. I was the first African American in the U.S. to what?
   A. Perform in movies
   B. Be a millionaire
   C. Have my own TV show

Directions: Answer the questions, to solve the crossword puzzle. You can use the internet if you get stuck on any question.

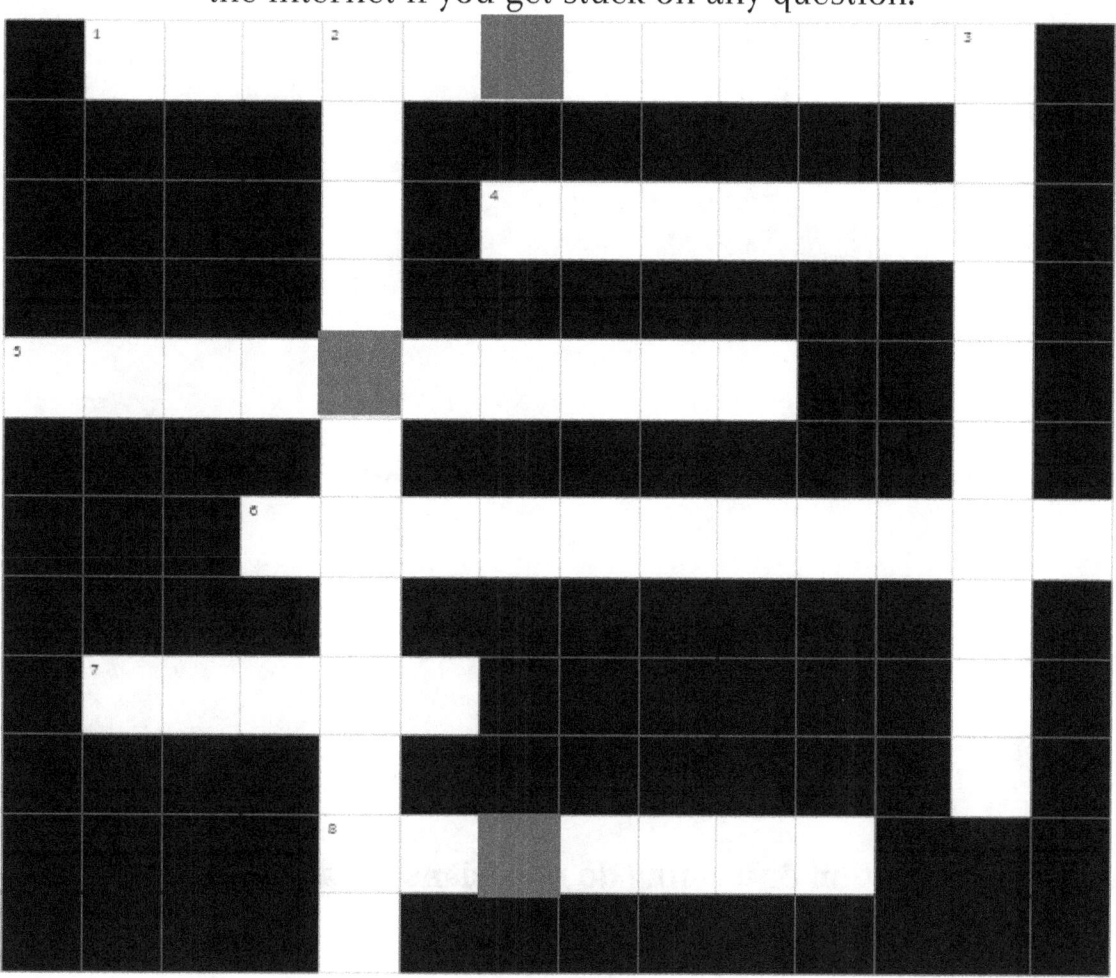

Across

1) Hazel refused to play the subservient roles in which _____ were commonly cast.
4) Hazel was known for "_____ the classics".
5) Hazel made her television acting debut in 1973, on the ABC daytime ____ One Life to Live.
6) Hazel was married to Baptist minister and US _____ Adam Clayton Powell.
7) Hazel moved to ____ in 1957 and began performing in Europe.
8) Hazel was the first black American to host her own _____.

Down

2) Hazel performed at _____ while still going to school.
3) Hazel refused to perform in ____ venues when she was on tour.

Directions: Read and answer the questions. These are your opinions so the answers will vary.

How do musicians write and create their own music?

What is the difference between a solo musician and a band?

What kind of education or training do musicians usually need to become successful?

Directions: Unscramble the words below about Hazel. See if you can get the bonus word.

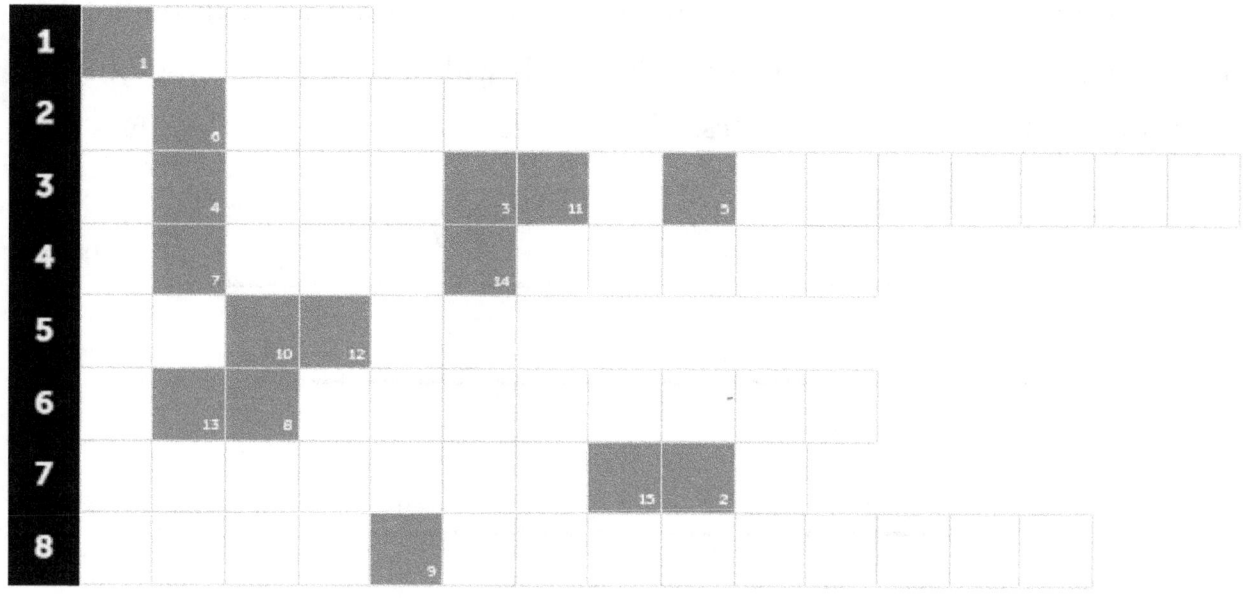

BONUS WORD

Unscramble Words

1) jzaz **2)** gsinre **3)** ctsaaicansslliip
4) cocseyfiate **5)** otshvw **6)** npsaotfripo
7) blcuototcn **8)** oaamwyrrbytdhh

Directions: This is the WGLT Challenge. Solve the cryptogram. As the puzzle solver, you need to find which number belongs to which character. And this can be pretty challenging! You will need to match the number with the letter. There are some letters given to you below. This will help you solve the other words and unlock more characters. **Good Luck.**

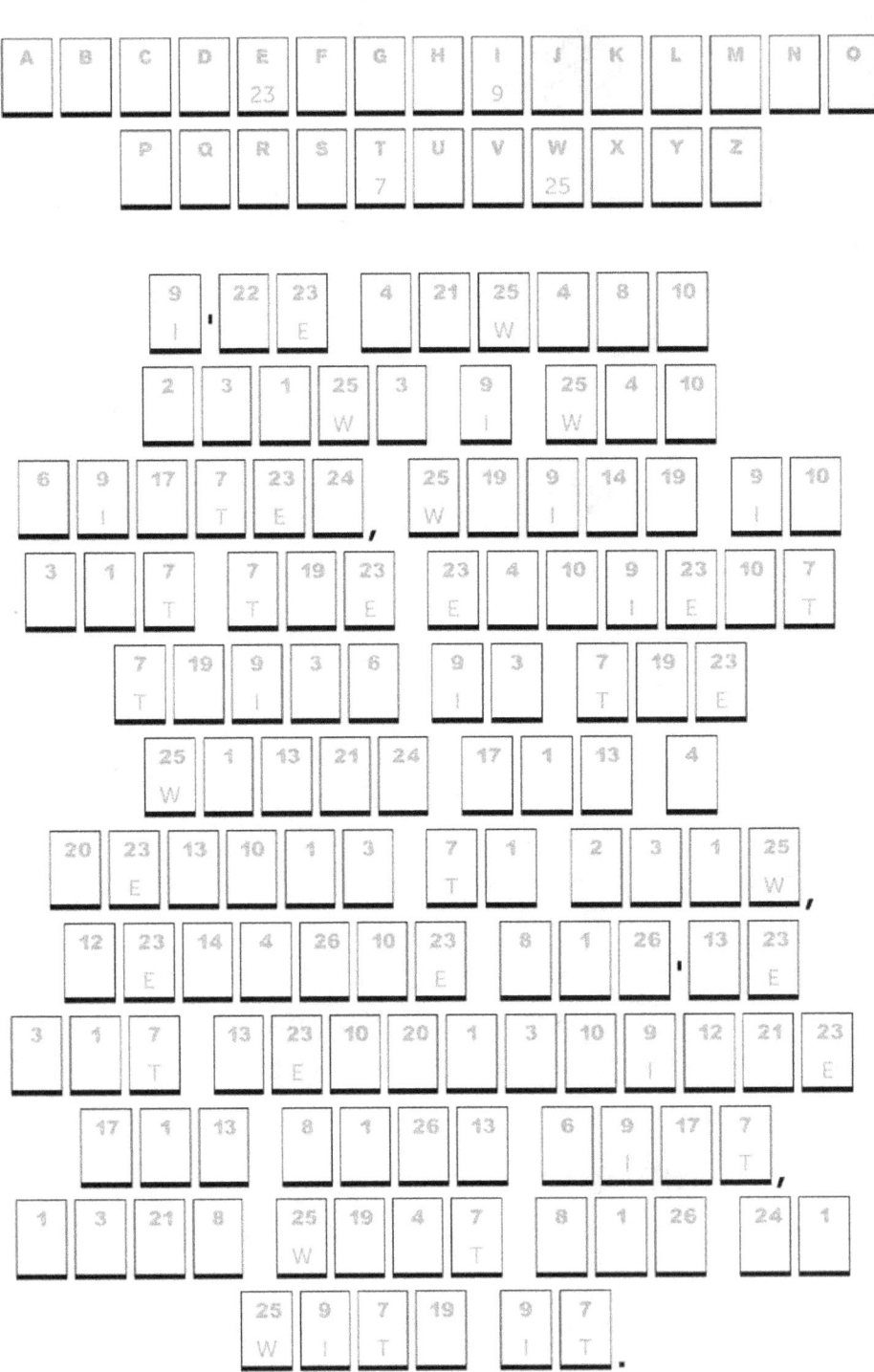

122

Lawrence Parker

Lawrence Parker

August 20, 1965 - PRESENT
RAPPER

123

LEFT BLANK ON PURPOSE

Lawrence Parker

Lawrence Parker

Lawrence Parker

Lawrence Parker

Lawrence Parker

Lawrence Parker

Directions: read the bio below and answer the following questions.

Hi, my name is Lawrence Parker. I was born on August 20, 1965, in Brooklyn, NY. I left home at 16 to become an emcee. I lived in a homeless shelter, which is where I met DJ Scott La Rock. I started going by KRS-One (Knowledge Reigns Supreme Over Nearly Everyone). In 1986, we started the group Boogie Down Productions (BDP). We released our debut album Criminal Minded in 1987. DJ Scott La Rock was killed later that year. I was determined to make BDP work after that. I released the album By All Means Necessary in 1988. In 1989, I started the Stop the Violence Movement, which was formed in response to violence in the hip hop and Black communities. I worked with many prominent emcees who appeared on the 12-inch single "Self-Destruction." Some of the songs I'm known for are "Sound of da Police," "Love's Gonna Get'cha (Material Love)," and "My Philosophy."

1. What year did I help found Boogie Down Productions?
   A. 1987
   B. 1986
   C. 1985
2. What movement did I start in response to violence?
   A. Stop the Violence Movement
   B. National Urban League
   C. NCAAP
3. I attracted many prominent emcees to appear on what?
   A. Tour
   B. Concert
   C. 12-inch single

126

Directions: Find the words associated with Lawrence's life and career.

```
Q V B I P F C U T O N X M Q O J C Z
C E G J O T S I C I R Y L T N L Y D
R G W D L P A C O F J X F R Y M O X
I A U G T T X G N B C U E H A N B P
M N O U I A F K D B I P U X U Z B G
I A R A P O A A W G P S C V D B M S
N C G A I K C O R A L T T O C S K I
A T W Z I R N R R J M V X J R F A M
L I J Y P B P R O D U C E R L G Y A
M V D B L B C M R U Z D C Y S A I M
I I T H E B R I D G E I S O V E R C
N S U Z Z K B M K W N F M H Q P T R
D T Y O O U E H S N U D A H O H Y U
E F T T A D U M H E U C M H Q K N 1
D F O Y Z P P W H X B Z P V A Q B 2
C Z Q K X Q F K J U A I X Y S R M K
C Q L A A W Y A Q J H Z Q M S Q S U
U T N O I T C U R T S E D F L E S V
```

Find These Words

HIPHOP   THEBRIDGEISOVER   SCOTTLAROCK
SELFDESTRUCTION   LYRICIST   PRODUCER
RAPPER   CRIMINALMINDED   VEGANACTIVIST

127

Directions: Read and answer the questions. These are your opinions so the answers will vary.

How do musicians come up with ideas for their songs, and what inspires them?

Can you name some famous musicians from different parts of the world, and what kind of music they play?

What is a music genre, and can you name some different types of genres?

Directions: Read and answer the questions below. There are clues in the puzzle to help you. Try and solve the cryptic message.

Clue for cryptic message: Lawrence appearance on a band song.

Questions

1) Lawrence was the Vice-President of A&R at Reprise _____ in 1999.
2) Lawrence authored a book called "The Gospel of Hip Hop: The First _".
3) People believe the live performance between Lawrence and MC Shan to be the first MC _____ where rappers attack each other.
4) Lawrence started the Stop the _____ Movement trying to end the violence in African-American communities.
5) Lawrence made his debut in his _____ in 1988 as himself in the movie "I'm Gonna Git You Sucka".
6) Lawrence _____ album was Criminal Minded in 1987.
7) Lawrence signed with Jive/RCA Records after his _____ album.
8) Lawrence founded the _____ of Hiphop, an organization to preserve and promote "Hiphop Kulture".
9) Lawrence use to be _____ in the street art activity graffiti.

Directions: This is the WGLT Challenge. Solve the cryptogram. As the puzzle solver, you need to find which number belongs to which character. And this can be pretty challenging! You will need to match the number with the letter. There are some letters given to you below. This will help you solve the other words and unlock more characters. **Good Luck.**

Ethel Waters

Ethel Waters

October 31, 1896 – September 1, 1977
SINGER / ACTRESS

131

LEFT BLANK ON PURPOSE

Ethel Waters

Ethel Waters

Ethel Waters

Ethel Waters

Ethel Waters

Ethel Waters

Directions: read the bio below and answer the following questions.

Hi, my name is Ethel Waters. I was born on October 31, 1896, in Chester, PA. When I was 17, I attended a costume party at a nightclub and I was persuaded to sing two songs. I impressed the audience so much that I was offered professional work at the Lincoln Theatre in Baltimore. I toured on the Black vaudeville circuit for a while. In 1919, I moved to Harlem and became a performer during the Harlem Renaissance. I recorded for Black Swan Records from 1921 through 1923. During this time, I also became the first Black woman to integrate Broadway's theater district, The Emperor Jones. In 1939, I became the first African American to star in my own TV show. In 1950, I became the first African American actress to star in a television series, Beulah, which aired on ABC television from 1950 through 1952. It was the first nationally broadcast weekly television series that starred an African American in a leading role. Some of the songs I'm known for are "Dinah," "Stormy Weather," "Taking a Chance on Love," and "Heat Wave."

1. I was the first African American in the U.S. to what?
    A. To star in a TV series
    B. To star in a movie
    C. To star in a play
2. What year did I move to Harlem?
    A. 1920
    B. 1918
    C. 1919
3. How did I get my start in music business?
    A. I sang in a Nightclub
    B. Talent Search
    C. Won a singing competition

Directions: Answer the questions, to solve the crossword puzzle. You can use the internet if you get stuck on any question.

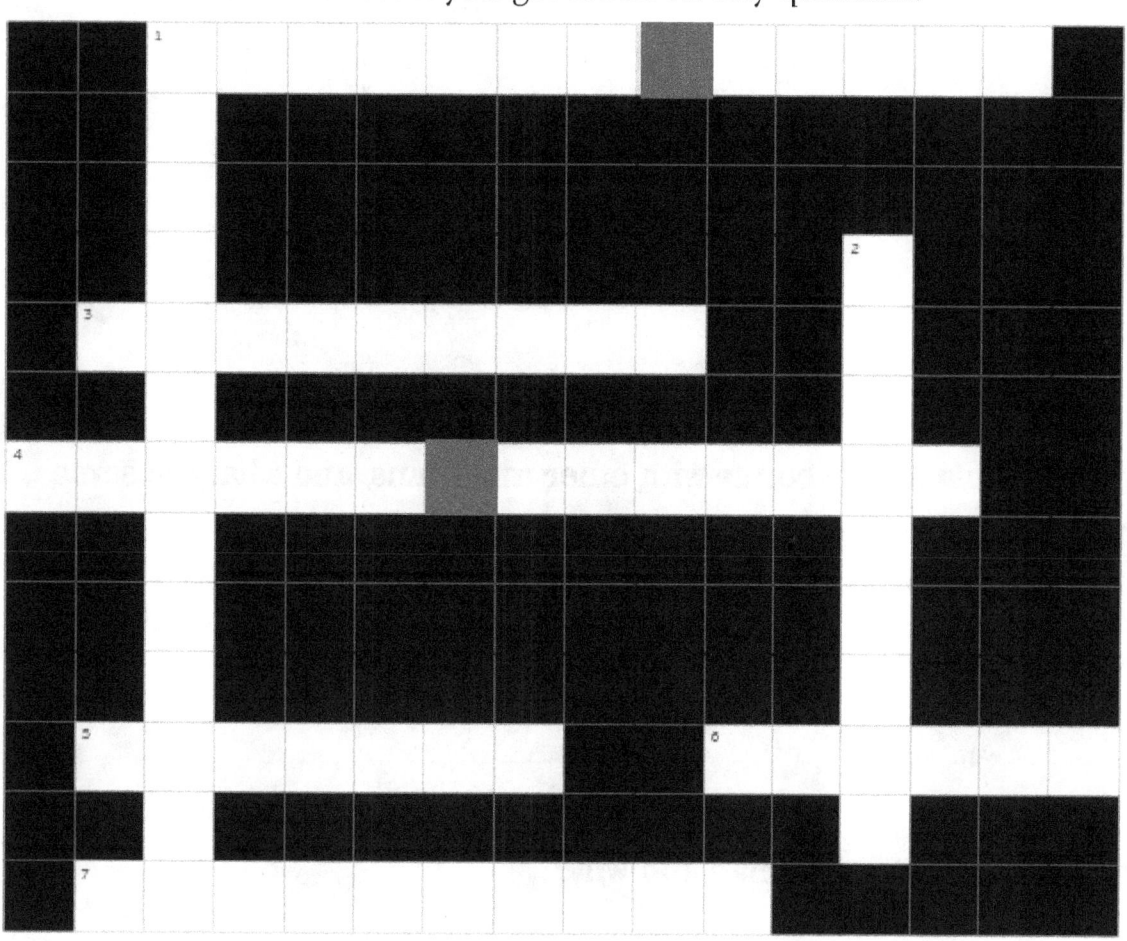

Across
1) Ethel won a New York Drama _____ in 1950 for her role in The Member of the Wedding.
3) In the 1930's, Ethel was the highest paid _____ of any race on Broadway.
4) Ethel's recording of "_____" (1933) was listed in the National Recording Registry by the National Recording Preservation Board of the Library of Congress in 2003.
5) Ethel made TV _____ when she became the first African-American woman to receive an Emmy nomination.
6) Ethel made history as the first black actress to star in a _____.
7) Ethel was one of the first African-Americans to appear on _____ in 1939.

Down
1) Postal Service issued a _____ stamp in Ethel's honor in September 1994.
2) Ethel was the first black actress to _____ a Broadway revue.

Directions: Read and answer the questions. These are your opinions so the answers will vary.

What are some important skills that musicians need to have in order to perform live on stage?

_____

_____

How do musicians collaborate with other musicians, and what are some examples of famous collaborations?

_____

_____

Who is your favorite musician and why?

_____

_____

_____

_____

Directions: Unscramble the words below about Ethel. See if you can get the bonus word.

BONUS WORD

1	2	3	4	5	6	7

Unscramble Words

1) scsarte
2) atywsmhertoer
3) snrige
4) zjza
5) brwadyoa
6) mpocisup
7) rambghailly

Directions: This is the WGLT Challenge. Solve the cryptogram. As the puzzle solver, you need to find which number belongs to which character. And this can be pretty challenging! You will need to match the number with the letter. There are some letters given to you below. This will help you solve the other words and unlock more characters. **Good Luck.**

September 25, 1968 - PRESENT
RAPPER / ACTOR / PRODUCER

139

Willard Carroll Smith II

Willard Carroll Smith II

Willard Carroll Smith II

Willard Carroll Smith II

Willard Carroll Smith II

Willard Carroll Smith II

Directions: read the bio below and answer the following questions.

Hi, my name is Willard Smith II. I was born on September 25, 1968, in Philadelphia, PA. In 1986, I graduated from Overbrook High School. Me and DJ Jazzy Jeff dropped our single "Girls Ain't Nothing but Trouble," which became our first hit a month before I graduated. In 1987, that song got us a record deal with Jive Records and Russell Simmons. In 1987, we debuted our first album Rock the House. We won the first Grammy Award for Best Rap Performance in 1989 for "Parents Just Don't Understand." In 1990, the NBC TV network signed me to a contract and built a sitcom, The Fresh Prince of Bel-Air, around me. In 1997, I started my solo music career by dropping my debut solo album, Big Willie Style. In the 90s, I started my movie career. Some of the movies I'm known for are Six Degrees of Separation (1993), Bad Boys (1995), Independence Day (1996) and Men in Black (1997).

1. What song was my first big hit?
   A. Parents Just Don't Understand
   B. Summertime
   C. Girls Ain't Nothing but Trouble
2. What year did we sign with Jive Records?
   A. 1987
   B. 1986
   C. 1990
3. Our group was the first rap group to what?
   A. Sell 10 million records
   B. Win a Grammy Award for Best Rap Performance
   C. Win a Grammy Award for Best Rap Album

Directions: Find the words associated with Will's life and career.

U	O	C	J	H	M	E	N	I	N	B	L	A	C	K	H	R	R
J	R	V	A	X	L	U	E	S	U	O	C	R	M	R	D	X	T
Z	I	Q	B	K	D	R	I	A	-	L	E	B	B	X	E	T	A
M	B	S	I	K	O	R	L	U	N	H	P	G	W	C	Y	Z	Q
K	A	V	K	B	A	C	C	W	F	T	W	Q	N	N	T	W	J
Z	D	S	I	X	H	S	Z	T	N	J	U	I	X	D	U	P	S
T	B	G	A	Y	P	Q	A	H	X	X	R	R	O	I	H	H	N
U	O	N	I	D	D	A	L	A	H	P	V	W	E	D	W	P	E
X	Y	V	D	X	O	V	Y	B	H	C	I	E	K	R	P	U	M
K	S	H	G	D	L	Y	K	S	G	A	K	Y	V	A	F	Q	I
H	C	F	X	N	K	W	E	A	W	M	J	B	A	W	W	N	T
B	N	V	Z	E	R	R	I	C	B	Y	V	M	R	A	T	I	R
P	R	F	S	D	F	E	F	T	A	A	B	A	N	Y	O	I	E
L	U	E	M	E	F	W	R	O	V	E	P	F	P	M	X	F	M
K	Y	F	H	E	O	C	J	R	U	P	Z	F	J	M	L	F	M
W	P	T	A	I	Q	T	Z	S	E	M	M	E	W	A	N	T	U
L	P	A	H	N	W	T	B	R	V	V	H	B	P	R	S	B	S
D	J	J	A	Z	Z	Y	J	E	F	F	B	T	D	G	M	S	B

Find These Words

THEFRESHPRINCE RAPPER BADBOYS
DJJAZZYJEFF ALADDIN ACTOR
MENINBLACK SUMMERTIME BEL-AIR
GRAMMYAWARD

143

Directions: Read and answer the questions. These are your opinions so the answers will vary.

What kind of instruments do musicians play?

What is your favorite song by a musician?

Can you name a musician from a different country or culture?

Directions: Read and answer the questions below. There are clues in the puzzle to help you. Try and solve the cryptic message.

Clue for cryptic message: Will's show.

Questions

1) Will starred in his _____ film "Where the Day Takes You" in 1992.
2) Will was already 6' 2" tall at _____ years old.
3) Will can _____ a Rubik's Cube in under fifty-five seconds.
4) Will is the only _____ to gross $100 million domestically with eight movies in a row.
5) Will became a _____ at the age of twenty.
6) Will's _____ is "Aw, hell no!"

Directions: This is the WGLT Challenge. Solve the cryptogram. As the puzzle solver, you need to find which number belongs to which character. And this can be pretty challenging! You will need to match the number with the letter. There are some letters given to you below. This will help you solve the other words and unlock more characters. **Good Luck.**

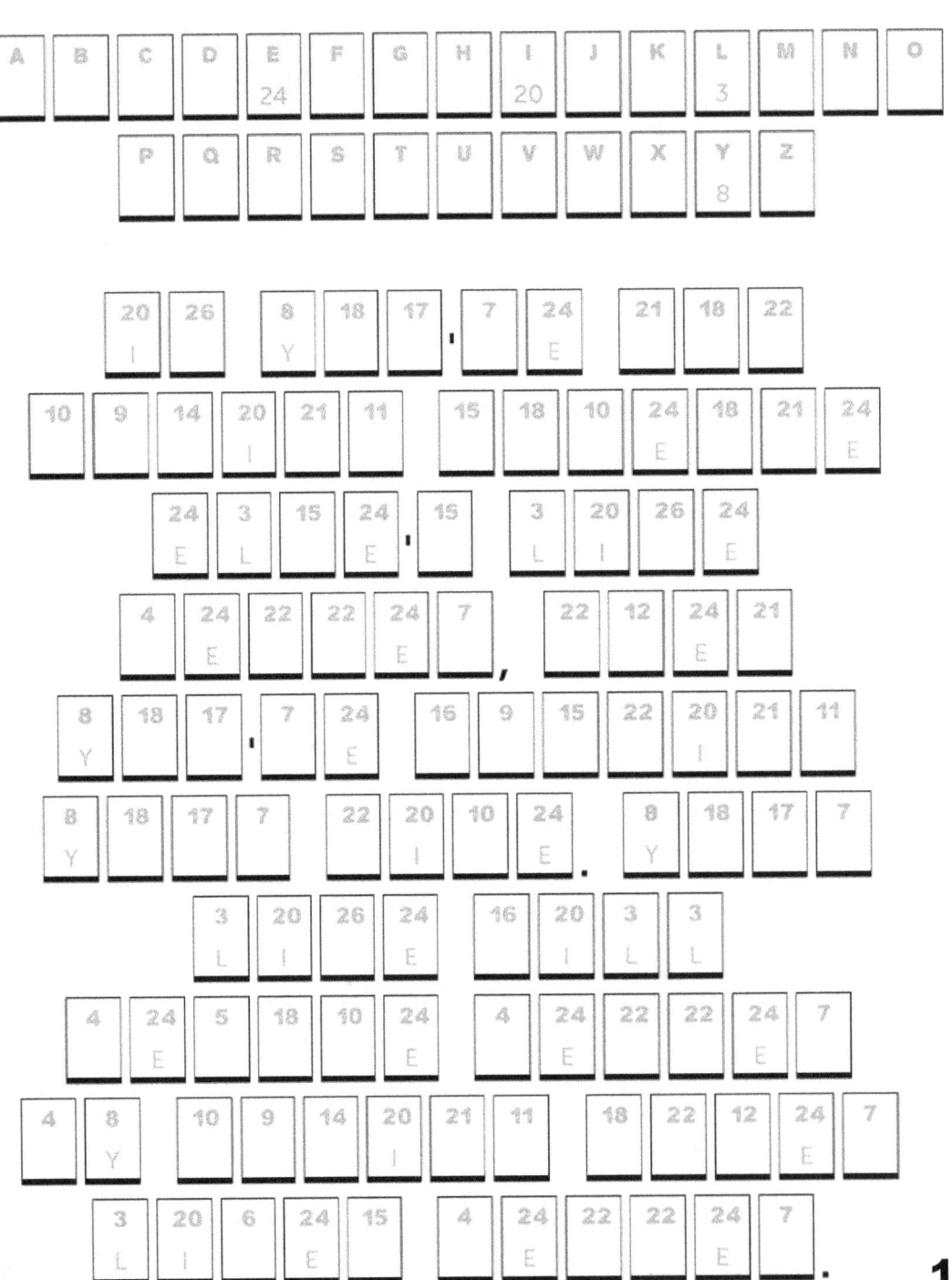

Anita Baker

January 26, 1958 - PRESENT
SINGER / SONGWRITER

Anita Baker

Anita Baker

Anita Baker

Anita Baker

Anita Baker

Anita Baker

Directions: read the bio below and answer the following questions.

Hi, my name is Anita Denise Baker. I was born on January 26, 1958, in Toledo, OH. When I was 16, I started singing in Detroit nightclubs. I joined a group called Chapter 8 in 1975. We toured for a while until we secured a record deal with Ariola Records in 1979. My first lead song was "I Just Want to Be Your Girl". Unfortunately, Arista Records bought Ariola and dropped us from the label. In 1983, I released my debut solo album, The Songstress. My best song from the album was "Angel." The new label Beverly Glen Music dragged their feet with my records and didn't give me my royalties, so I sued to get out of the contract. I won and then signed with Warner Music Group in 1985. In 1986, I released my second album, Rapture. It received a Platinum certification and I won two Grammy Awards for it. I collaborated with The Winans in 1987 on the song "Ain't No Need to Worry," which also helped me win my third Grammy. Some of the songs I'm known for are "Giving You the Best That I Got," "Just Because," "Sweet Love," and "Body and Soul."

1. What was the name of the band I started with?
   A. Chapter 5
   B. Chapter 8
   C. Chapter 3
2. What song brought me my third Grammy win?
   A. Angel
   B. Sweet Love
   C. Ain't No Need to Worry
3. What record label released the album Rapture?
   A. Warner Music Group
   B. Ariola
   C. Beverly Glen Music

Directions: Answer the questions, to solve the crossword puzzle. You can use the internet if you get stuck on any question.

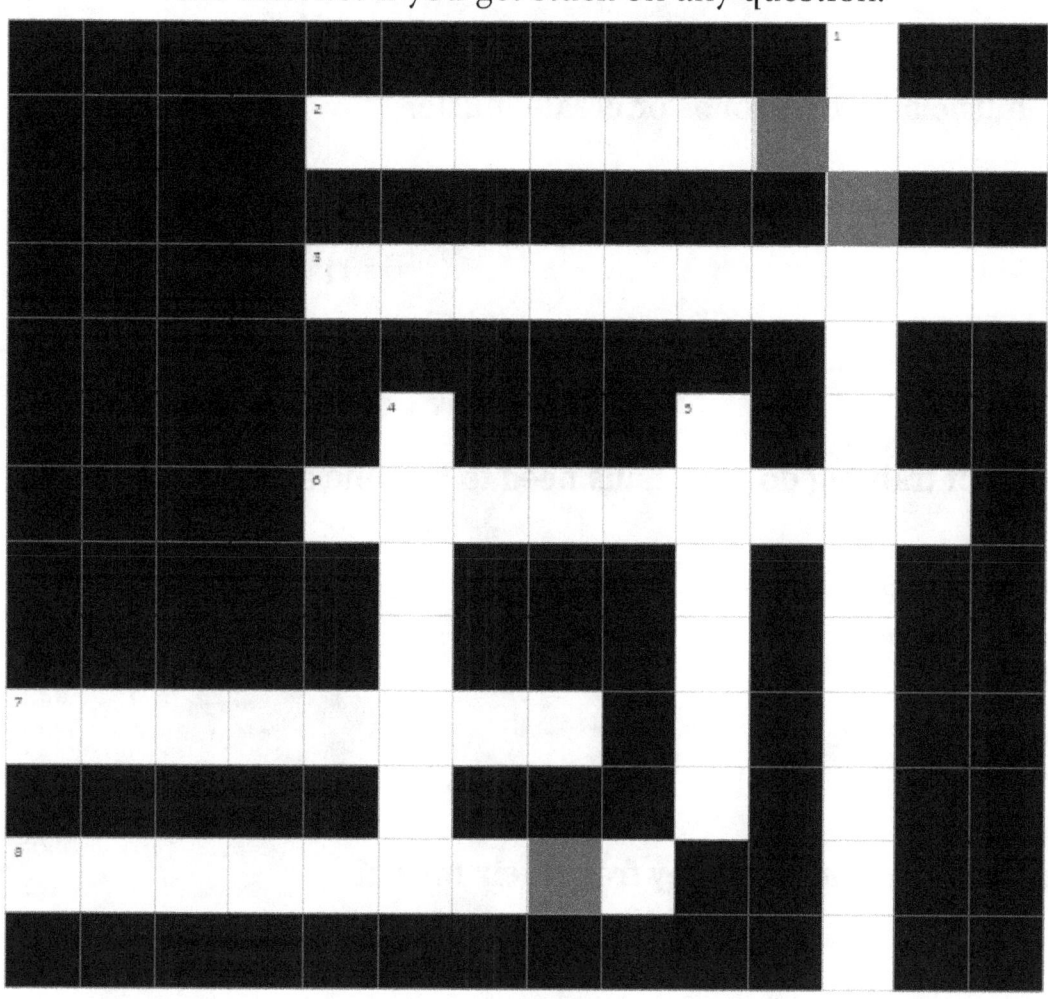

Across
2) Anita's song "_____ the Best That I Got", was a Top 5 single, which remains her highest charter to date
3) Anita released her debut album, The _____ in 1983.
6) Anita spent 109 weeks on the _____ hot 100 during the 1980's, making her one of the most consistent R&B singers of the decade.
7) Anita has five _____ albums under her belt.
8) Anita started her career in the late 1970s with the funk band ___.

Down
1) Anita released her last studio album "_____," in 2004.
4) Anita adopted a class of Detroit high school students and later helped ___ their college education.
5) Anita began singing in the ____ choir.

Directions: Read and answer the questions. These are your opinions so the answers will vary.

How do musicians write songs or create music?

_____

_____

What kind of training do musicians need to become successful?

_____

_____

How do musicians make money from their music?

_____

_____

_____

_____

_____

Directions: Unscramble the words below about Anita. See if you can get the bonus word.

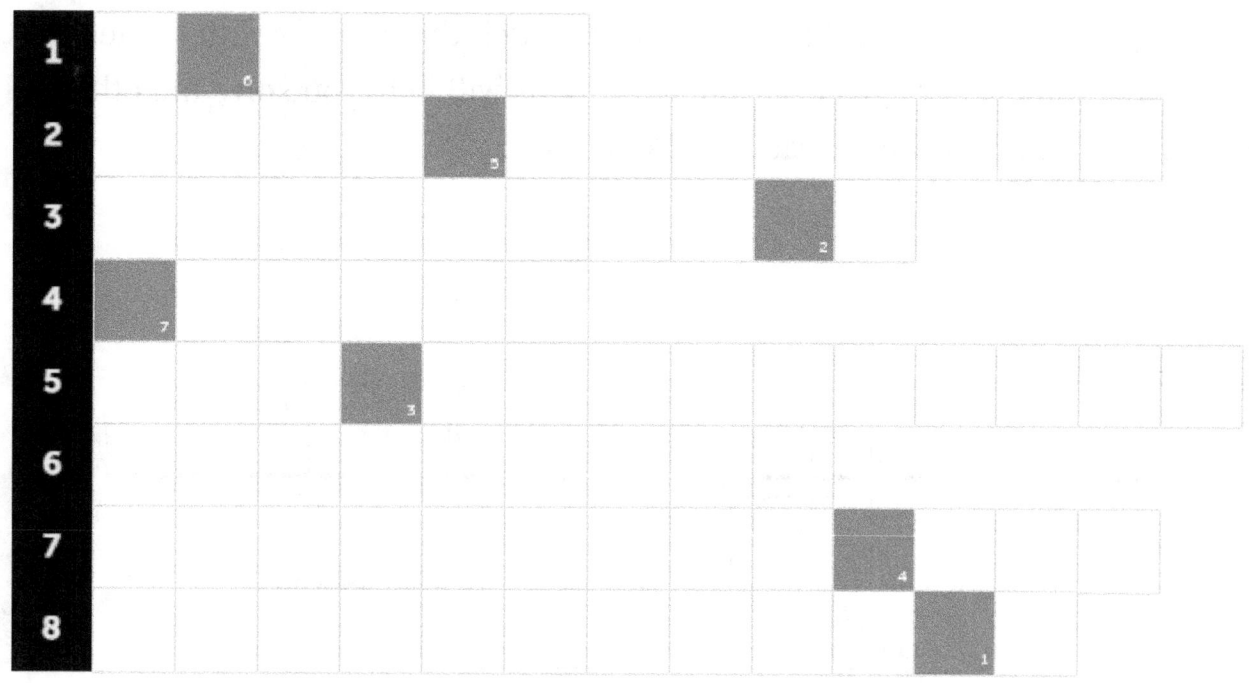

BONUS WORD

Unscramble Words

1) rneisg
2) nsghrtosseste
3) ergoirtnws
4) dlteoo
5) mtabuulpnsialm
6) vleseowte
7) zraoo-epnsmoz
8) adsaraygrwmm

Directions: This is the WGLT Challenge. Solve the cryptogram. As the puzzle solver, you need to find which number belongs to which character. And this can be pretty challenging! You will need to match the number with the letter. There are some letters given to you below. This will help you solve the other words and unlock more characters. **Good Luck.**

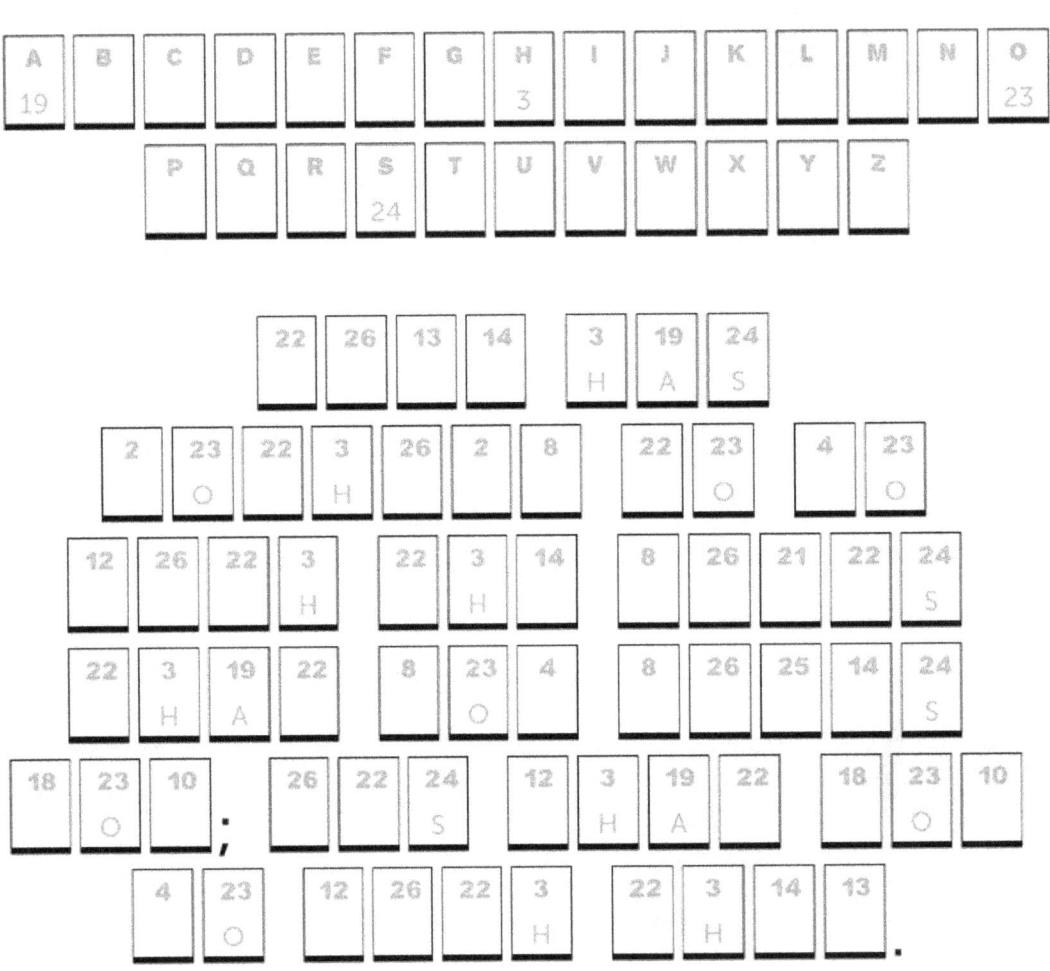

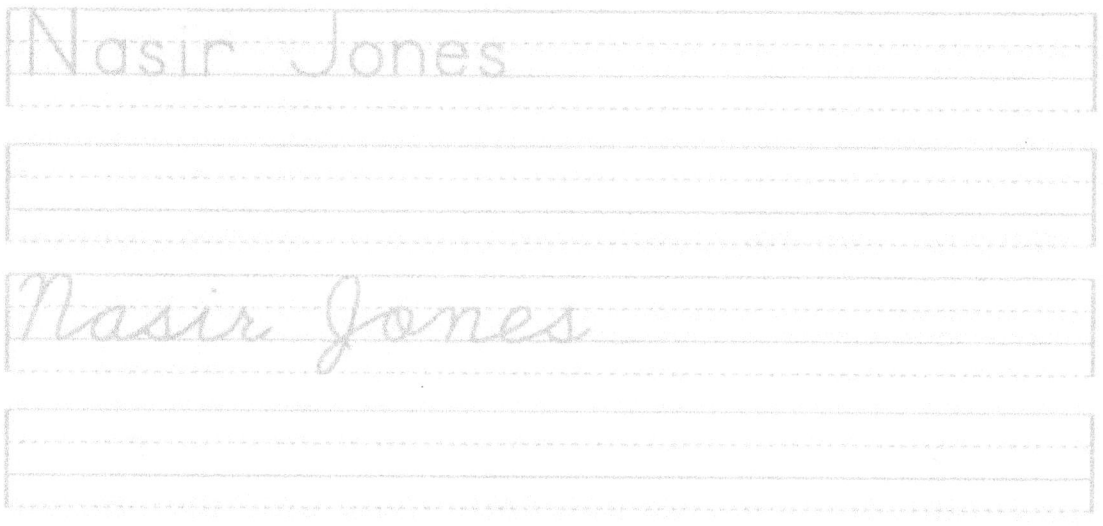

September 14, 1973 - PRESENT
RAPPER   **155**

LEFT BLANK ON PURPOSE

Nasir Jones

Nasir Jones

Nasir Jones

Nasir Jones

Nasir Jones

Nasir Jones

Directions: read the bio below and answer the following questions.

Hi, my name is Nasir bin Olu Dara Jones. I was born on May 26, 1926, in Brooklyn, NY. I would like to tell you a little bit about my name, "Nasir": it is an Arabic name that means "helper and protector," while "bin" means "son of" in Arabic. When I was just a young teen, my alias was "Kid Wave." By the time I had my first big performance in 1991 at Main Source's Live at the Barbeque, I became known as "Nasty Nas," or "Nas" for short. In 1992, I signed with Columbia Records and shortly after, in 1994, I released my debut album, Illmatic. Some have said that it is the greatest hip-hop album of all time. In 1996, I followed up with my second album, It Was Written. The biggest singles that I released were "If I Ruled the World (Imagine That)" (which featured Lauryn Hill of The Fugees) and "Street Dreams" (which included a remix with R. Kelly). One of the things I'm best known for is blending poetry with jazz. Some of the songs I'm known for are "I Can," "Nas Is Like," "N.Y. State of Mind," and "Daughters."

1. What was my first stage name?
   A. Nasty Nas
   B. Nas
   C. Kid Wave
2. What year did I drop arguably the best hip hop album?
   A. 1996
   B. 1994
   C. 1992
3. Which song is not one of mine?
   A. New York State of Mind
   B. If I Ruled the World
   C. Empire State of Mind

Directions: Find the words associated with Nas's life and career.

M	K	L	N	G	N	D	C	V	A	R	O	G	E	T	J	B	T
W	Y	R	S	Y	J	P	E	Z	A	I	M	M	V	G	K	M	I
Z	K	I	K	W	Q	O	R	P	S	T	S	I	C	I	R	I	L
D	M	J	V	G	S	P	P	Y	A	T	V	Q	K	M	C	H	Z
Z	K	W	R	G	J	E	O	C	P	C	M	J	X	H	G	Q	E
K	G	V	C	O	R	P	Q	I	Y	X	D	U	I	C	G	J	O
S	A	X	A	J	K	G	R	A	M	M	Y	A	W	A	R	D	G
I	N	T	O	O	D	E	E	P	J	I	Z	G	J	T	Q	N	G
L	W	R	R	V	M	Q	R	S	M	X	H	U	H	E	G	O	E
N	I	H	E	A	B	N	J	J	O	E	P	V	P	L	D	G	O
C	J	L	H	L	A	U	R	Y	N	H	I	L	L	S	T	C	S
T	B	A	L	H	K	E	N	R	S	C	B	N	S	B	H	I	C
E	H	U	T	M	F	P	J	A	T	C	Z	O	J	Y	J	M	V
P	I	N	H	Y	A	D	A	B	E	I	N	F	K	H	D	E	L
J	V	M	S	N	D	T	A	N	R	K	W	N	S	Z	Y	N	R
S	B	I	Y	I	S	B	I	R	A	C	B	Q	X	J	R	O	B
I	N	D	U	V	R	F	H	C	K	E	R	E	I	G	V	Q	L
M	A	S	S	A	P	P	E	A	L	R	E	C	O	R	D	S	E

Find These Words

RAPPER
GRAMMYAWARD
GODSSON
MASSAPPEALRECORDS

ILLMATIC
INTOODEEP
MONSTER

LAURYNHILL
ONEMIC
LIRICISTS

Directions: Read and answer the questions. These are your opinions so the answers will vary.

What are some of the challenges that musicians face in their careers?

How has technology changed the way musicians create and share their music?

What are some popular genres of music, and who are some famous musicians in those genres?

Directions: Read and answer the questions below. There are clues in the puzzle to help you. Try and solve the cryptic message.

Clue for cryptic message: Nas's nickname.

Questions

1) Nas's album "_____ Disease," won him his first Grammy for Best Rap Album.

2) Nas's debut album _____ is considered to be one of the greatest hip hop albums of all time.

3) Nas's father, Olu _____, is a jazz and blues musician.

4) Nas's album Illmatic was _____ best album of 1994 by The Source Magazine.

5) Nas career began in 1989 as he adopted the moniker of "_____ Nas".

6) Nas was _____ in a highly publicized feud with the rapper Jay-Z.

7) Nas film debut was in the movie _____.

Directions: This is the WGLT Challenge. Solve the cryptogram. As the puzzle solver, you need to find which number belongs to which character. And this can be pretty challenging! You will need to match the number with the letter. There are some letters given to you below. This will help you solve the other words and unlock more characters. **Good Luck.**

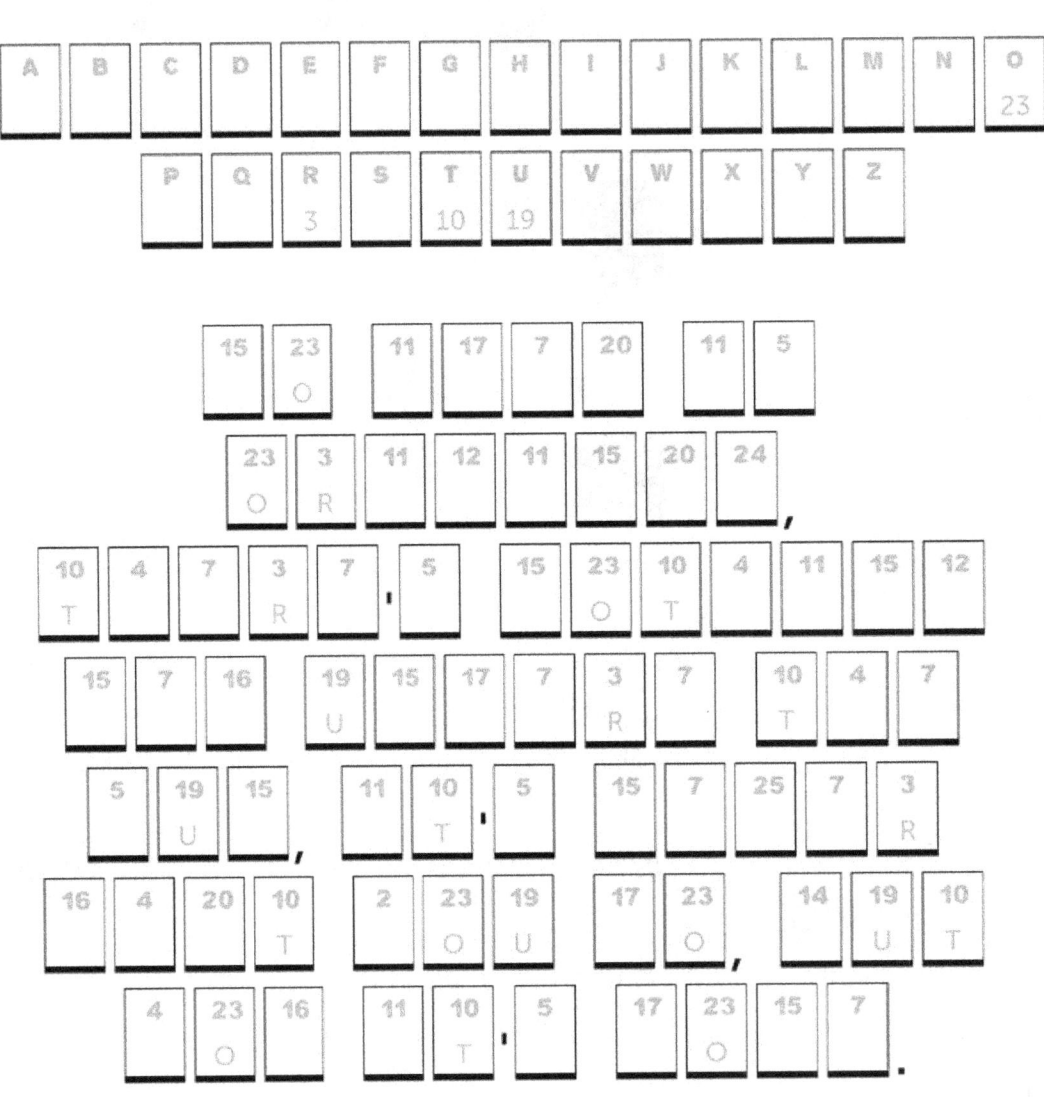

162

Pearl Bailey

Pearl Bailey

163

March 29, 1918 – August 17, 1990
WSINGER / ACTRESS

LEFT BLANK ON PURPOSE

Pearl Bailey

Pearl Bailey

Pearl Bailey

Pearl Bailey

Pearl Bailey

Pearl Bailey

Directions: read the bio below and answer the following questions.

Hi, my name is Pearl Mae Bailey. I was born on March 29, 1918, in Newport News, VA. I graduated from Booker T. Washington High School. Later in life, when I was 67 years old, I graduated from Georgetown University with a degree in theology. When I was 15, I won an amateur contest at the Pearl Theatre and later won another contest at the Apollo Theater. That's when I decided to pursue music as a career. I started singing and dancing in Philadelphia's Black nightclubs in the 1930s. During World War II, in 1941, I toured the country with the USO and performed for American troops. In 1946, I made my Broadway debut in St. Louis Woman and I won a Donaldson Award for being the best Broadway newcomer. Cab Calloway and I headlined an all-Black cast version of Hello, Dolly in 1967. In 1971, I hosted my own variety series on ABC, The Pearl Bailey Show. Some of the movies and tv shows that I'm known for are Carmen Jones, St. Louis Blues, The Fox and the Hound, Carl Channing, The Muppet Show, Hello, Dolly and Tubby the Tuba.

1. What college did I graduate from?
    A. Temple University
    B. Georgetown University
    C. New York University
2. What year did I host The Pearl Bailey Show?
    A. 1971
    B. 1867
    C. 1974
3. I won amateur contest at what Theatre?
    A. Earle Theatre
    B. Mastbaum Theatre
    C. Pearl Theatre

Directions: Answer the questions, to solve the crossword puzzle. You can use the internet if you get stuck on any question.

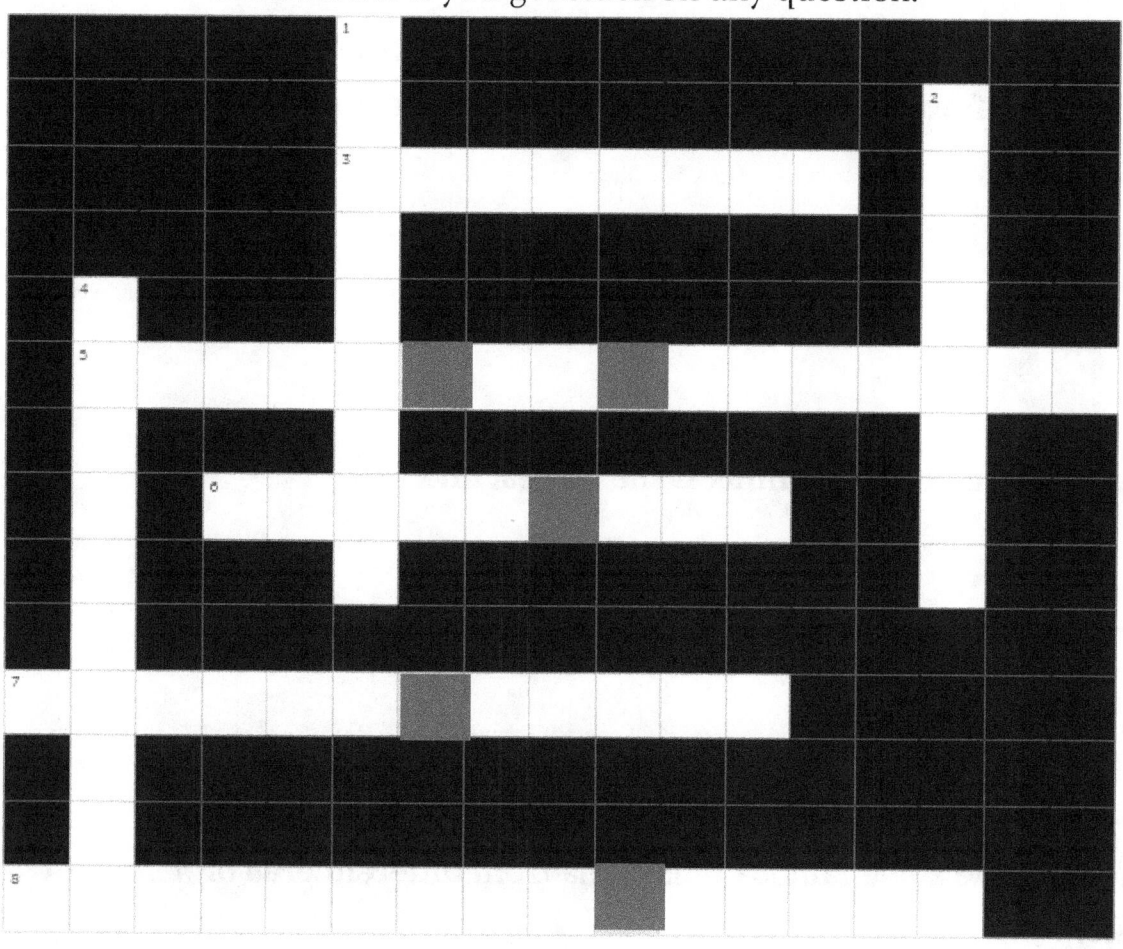

Across

3) Pearl sang with jazz stars like Cab _____ and Duke Ellington.
5) Pearl received the Presidential _____.
6) Pearl toured nationally with the USO during ____ II.
7) In 1954, Pearl made her film debut in _____.
8) Pearl was appointed by _____ as the nation's "Ambassador of Love" in 1970.

Down

1) It took Pearl seven years to earn her _____ degree.
2) Pearl made her _____ debut in 1946 in St. Louis Woman alongside Mahalia Jackson, Eartha Kitt and Nat King Cole.
4) Pearl was appointed special _____ to the United Nations by President Ford.

Directions: Read and answer the questions. These are your opinions so the answers will vary.

Who is your favorite musician and why do you like them?

What instrument do you think is the coolest and why?

Can you name some famous musicians from different eras or genres of music?

Directions: Unscramble the words below about Pearl. See if you can get the bonus word.

BONUS WORD

Unscramble Words

1) taesrsc
2) netaootottwgaks
3) risegn
4) lyaiibblel
5) rahtou
6) doefsoldlbi
7) alpcieurnb
8) aybwaodr

Directions: This is the WGLT Challenge. Solve the cryptogram. As the puzzle solver, you need to find which number belongs to which character. And this can be pretty challenging! You will need to match the number with the letter. There are some letters given to you below. This will help you solve the other words and unlock more characters. **Good Luck.**

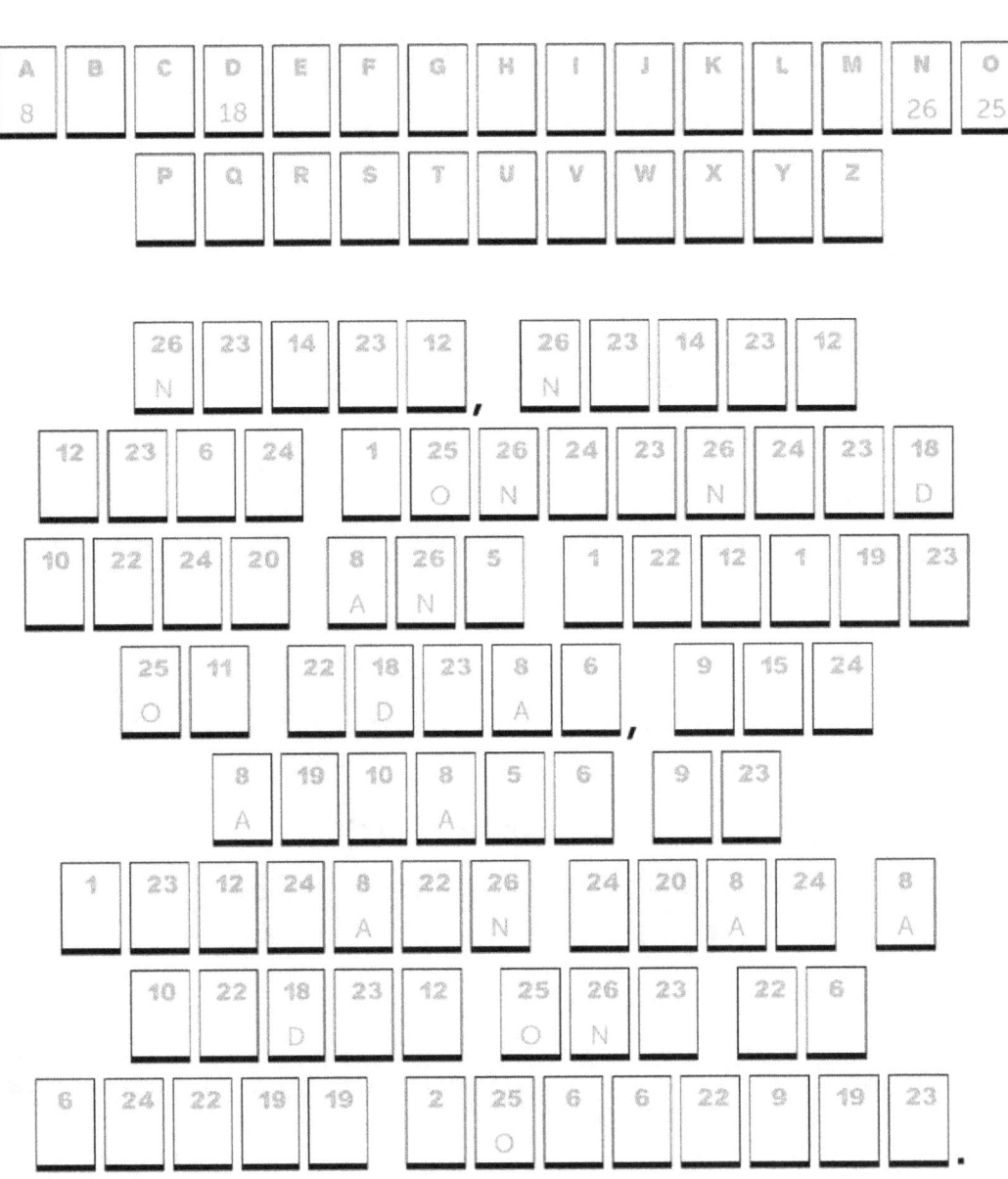

170

Beyoncé Knowles

Beyoncé Knowles

September 4, 1981 - PRESENT
SINGER / SONGWRITER

171

LEFT BLANK ON PURPOSE

Beyoncé Knowles

Beyoncé Knowles

Beyoncé Knowles

Beyoncé Knowles

Beyoncé Knowles

Beyoncé Knowles

Directions: read the bio below and answer the following questions.

Hi, my name is Beyoncé Knowles. I was born on September 4, 1981, in Houston, TX. I attended the High School for the Performing and Visual Arts. When I began my career, I was in a group called Girl's Tyme with three other girls and rapped and danced on the talent show circuit in Houston. We got to perform in Star Search but didn't win. We signed with Columbia Records in 1996. We changed our name to Destiny's Child and released our debut album, Destiny's Child, in 1998. We released our second album, The Writing's on the Wall, in 1999. Both albums were later Platinum certified. In 2003, I released my first solo album, Dangerously in Love. In 2006, I starred in The Pink Panther and Dreamgirls. In 2008, I starred in Cadillac Records. I'm the first solo artist to have my first six studio albums debut at number one on the Billboard 200. Some of the songs that I'm known for are "Formation," "Crazy in Love," "Single Ladies," and "Get Me Bodied."

1. What was the name of my group when I first started?
    A. Destiny's Child
    B. En Vogue
    C. Girl's Tyme
2. What year did I release my debut solo album?
    A. 1996
    B. 2003
    C. 2000
3. I was the first solo artist to do what?
    A. Have six studio albums debut at number one
    B. Have six studio albums go platinum
    C. Have six studio albums debut at number one overseas

Directions: Find the words associated with Beyoncé's life and career.

U	Y	Y	Z	M	A	W	J	S	E	M	P	L	W	X	X	W	P
L	D	C	G	R	A	M	M	Y	A	W	A	R	D	S	D	I	R
C	R	A	Z	Y	I	N	L	O	V	E	Q	T	I	E	B	W	I
U	W	Y	D	C	F	I	Y	C	U	K	E	J	S	L	A	D	S
P	R	O	D	U	C	E	R	Q	N	T	L	T	P	A	A	R	S
M	H	L	Y	Y	B	I	B	F	X	T	I	C	H	H	M	E	E
E	Y	G	U	B	R	U	M	C	T	N	V	I	I	U	V	A	R
U	X	M	E	O	W	E	E	G	Y	X	R	R	L	A	E	M	T
O	M	C	G	L	S	B	G	S	I	T	U	P	A	A	A	G	C
J	U	P	Z	W	V	Y	C	N	K	G	D	C	N	X	R	I	A
M	E	H	P	P	A	H	M	X	I	X	D	Q	T	M	U	R	C
F	U	R	E	S	I	I	M	K	I	S	O	O	H	V	H	L	O
W	X	T	T	L	I	X	I	P	A	J	K	I	R	O	K	S	U
N	X	U	D	R	X	I	H	Y	O	E	J	D	O	P	Z	D	B
X	G	B	U	S	Z	V	L	L	O	T	R	Z	P	N	A	J	P
M	U	U	D	U	B	Y	Z	R	J	A	E	B	Y	N	L	G	M
I	S	O	N	G	W	R	I	T	E	R	T	Z	I	V	X	X	Q
M	X	P	D	I	B	F	B	Z	C	O	B	P	L	I	R	Z	K

Find These Words

PHILANTHROPY SINGER DESTINYSCHILD
DREAMGIRLS PRODUCER SONGWRITER
GRAMMYAWARDS CRAZYINLOVE ACTRESS
BREAKMYSOUL

Directions: Read and answer the questions. These are your opinions so the answers will vary.

How do musicians write and create their music?

How do musicians practice and improve their skills?

What is your favorite song and why do you like it?

Directions: Read and answer the questions below. There are clues in the puzzle to help you. Try and solve the cryptic message.

Clue for cryptic message: Beyoncé fans.

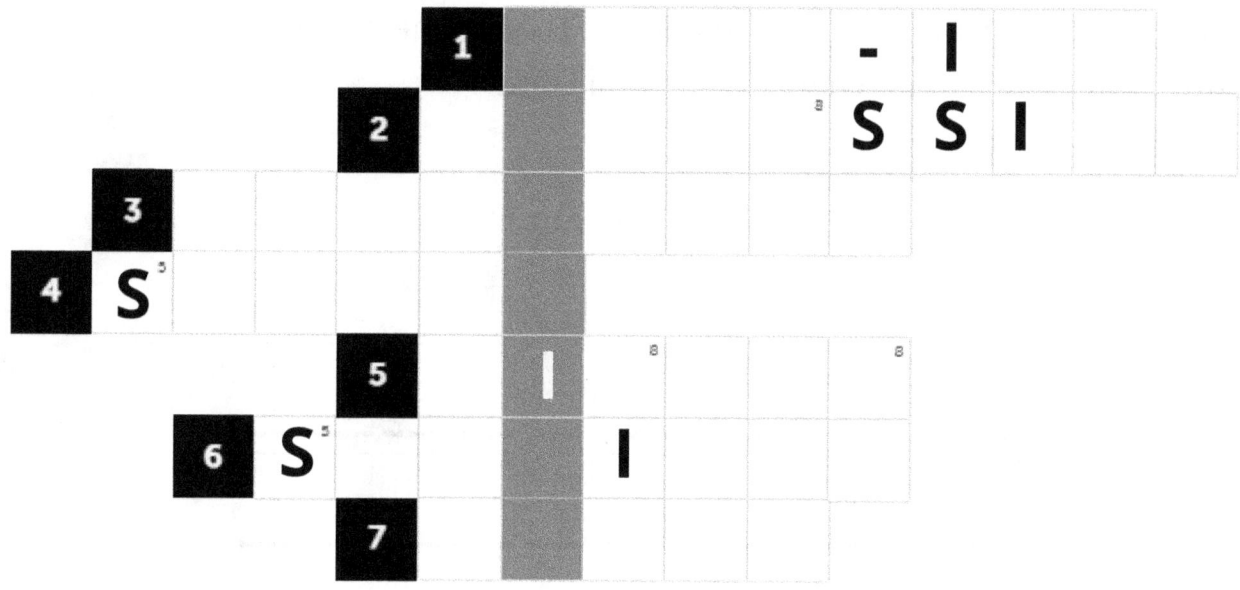

Questions

1) Beyoncé's daughter _____ Carter is the youngest charted recording artist in history.

2) Beyoncé suffered from _____ for two years after Destiny's Child broke up in 2006.

3) Beyoncé accepted a star on the _____ Walk of Fame in 2006.

4) Beyoncé competed on the competition series "Star __" in 1993.

5) Beyoncé has an on-stage alter ego, named Sasha _____.

6) Beyoncé co-founded a relief foundation called _____ Foundation.

7) Beyoncé's vocal range spans 3.6 octaves and is classified as __-soprano.

Directions: This is the WGLT Challenge. Solve the cryptogram. As the puzzle solver, you need to find which number belongs to which character. And this can be pretty challenging! You will need to match the number with the letter. There are some letters given to you below. This will help you solve the other words and unlock more characters. **Good Luck.**

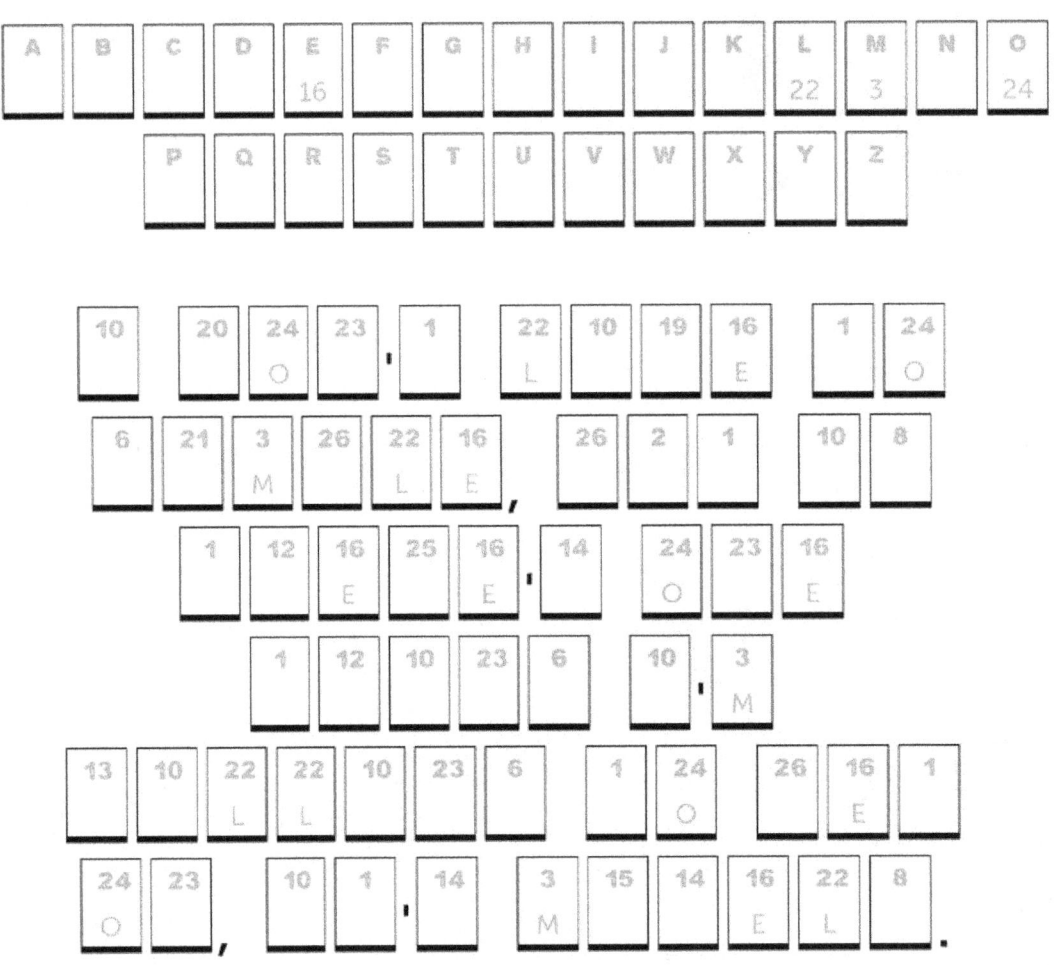

4 March 1932 – 9 November 2008
SOUTH AFRICAN SINGER

LEFT BLANK ON PURPOSE

Zenzile Miriam Makeba

Zenzile Miriam Makeba

Zenzile Miriam Makeba

Zenzile Miriam Makeba

Zenzile Miriam Makeba

Zenzile Miriam Makeba

Directions: read the bio below and answer the following questions.

Hi, my name is Zenzile Miriam Makeba. I was born on March 4, 1932, in Johannesburg, Union of South Africa. My talent for singing was noticed when I was about 8, which is when I was in the choir at the Kilnerton Training Institute. I sang in church choirs in English, Xhosa, Sotho and Zulu. I learned to sing in English before I could speak the language. I started my career with the Cuban Brothers, but after I turned 21, I joined the Manhattan Brothers, who sang a mixture of South African songs and pieces from popular African American groups. I recorded my first hit, "Laku Tshoni Ilanga," in 1953 and developed a national reputation as a musician. In 1956, I joined a new all-woman group, the Skylarks. I sang a blend of jazz and traditional South African melodies. I released my first solo success, "Lovely Lies," which became the first South African record to chart on the United States Billboard Top 100. Two of the names I'm best known by are "Mama Africa" and the "Empress of African Song."

1. What age did they realize my gift with singing?
    A. 6
    B. 10
    C. 8
2. What year did I find a national reputation?
    A. 1953
    B. 1960
    C. 1956
3. I was the first South African to do what in the U.S.?
    A. Do a Broadway Play
    B. Make the Billboard Top 100
    C. Star in an U.S. movie

Directions: Answer the questions, to solve the crossword puzzle. You can use the internet if you get stuck on any question.

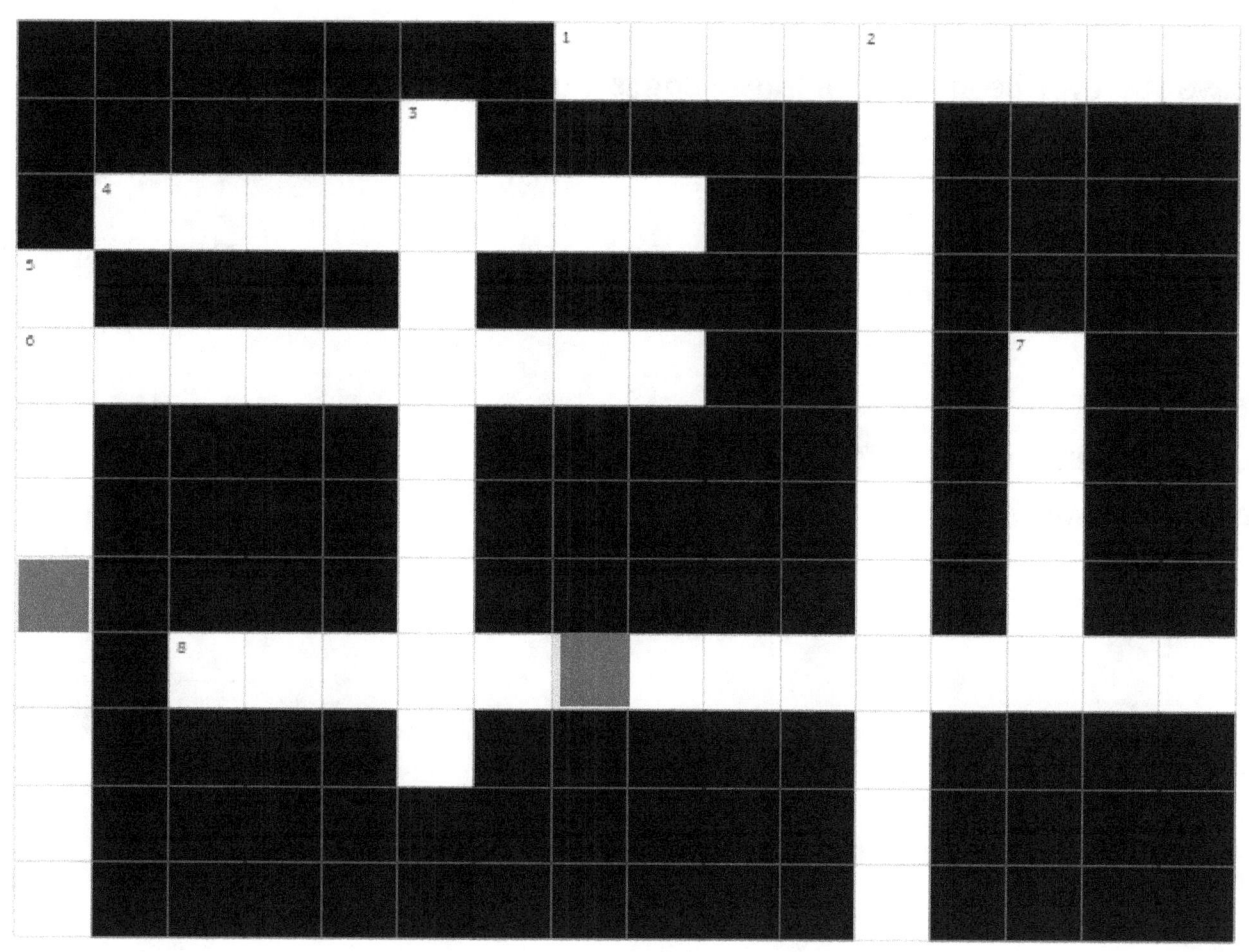

Across
1) Miriam was married Stokely _____, a leader of the Black Panther Party.
4) Miriam was in an all-woman group, the _____, performing a mixture of jazz, traditional African melodies and Western popular music.
6) Miriam testified against South Africa's _____ government.
8) Miriam sang covers of popular American songs with The _____.

Down
2) Miriam sang at the _____ of the Organization of African Unity.
3) Miriam recorded her first hit, "Laku Tshoni Ilanga" with the _____ brothers.
5) Miriam most popular song was "_____."
7) Miriam began her career performing ____, a style of vocal harmony which drew on American jazz, ragtime and Anglican church hymns

Directions: Read and answer the questions. These are your opinions so the answers will vary.

Have you ever been to a live music concert or performance? How was it?

_____

_____

Can you name some different types of music and describe their characteristics?

_____

_____

What are some popular musical instruments and how are they played?

_____

_____

_____

_____

_____

Directions: Unscramble the words below about Zenzile. See if you can get the bonus word.

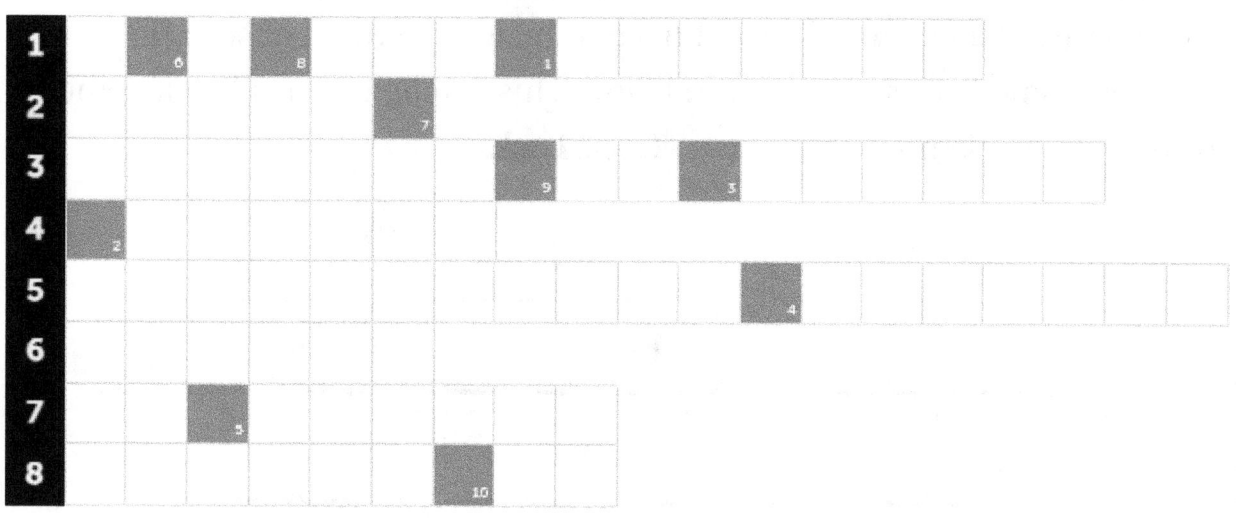

BONUS WORD

1	2	3	4		5	6	7	8	9	10

Unscramble Words

1) acdmnisiaeolfre **2)** sgrien **3)** sathomcerelkiaylc
4) strcase **5)** gvichtilarsitisitcv **6)** oldonn
7) hpeaadrti **8)** at-ptapaa

Directions: This is the WGLT Challenge. Solve the cryptogram. As the puzzle solver, you need to find which number belongs to which character. And this can be pretty challenging! You will need to match the number with the letter. There are some letters given to you below. This will help you solve the other words and unlock more characters. **Good Luck.**

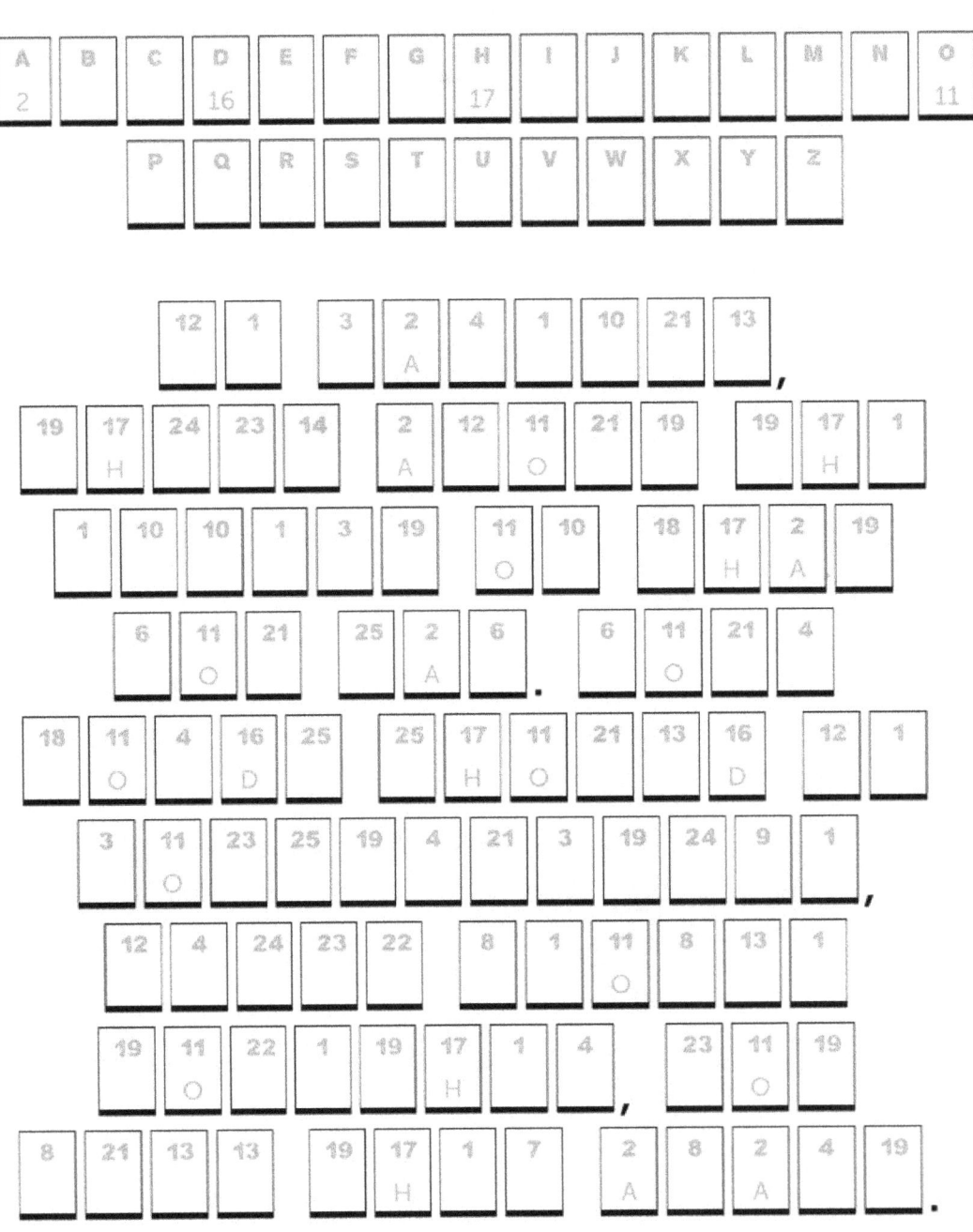

186

February 27, 1897 – April 8, 1993
CONTRALTO

187

Marian Anderson

Marian Anderson

Marian Anderson

Marian Anderson

Marian Anderson

Marian Anderson

Directions: read the bio below and answer the following questions.

Hi, my name is Marian Anderson. I was born on February 27, 1897, in Philadelphia, PA. I started singing in the junior church choir. when I was about 6. I started singing for local functions when I turned 10. I later joined the People's Chorus of Philadelphia and I was often a soloist. I graduated from South Philadelphia High School in 1921. I tried to enroll in the Philadelphia Music Academy (which is now the University of the Arts) but was denied because I was Black. I recorded "Deep River" and "My Way's Cloudy" in 1923. In 1925, I won a singing competition. I got to perform in concert with an orchestra in 1925. I held my first performance at Carnegie Hall in 1928. Because of Jim Crow laws, I had to go to Europe to be able to tour. I came back to the US in 1934, but in 1939, the Daughters of the American Revolution (DAR) denied me permission to hold a concert at Constitution Hall because of a "white performers only" policy that was in effect at the time. One of the things I'm best known for is becoming the first African American to sing with the Metropolitan Opera in New York.

1. **What song is not one of mine?**
   A. **Deep River**
   B. **My Ways Cloudy**
   C. **Caravan**
2. **What age did I start doing solo acts?**
   A. **6**
   B. **10**
   C. **21**
3. **What policy denied me permission for a concert?**
   A. **Crowd size policy**
   B. **White performers-only policy**
   C. **Bag policy**

Directions: Find the words associated with Marian's life and career.

R	E	A	T	C	D	L	W	Z	W	X	N	Q	L	H	U	G	R
A	A	L	M	T	N	C	P	M	Q	D	O	I	A	I	C	U	R
C	K	N	E	G	M	I	H	P	H	A	R	G	R	S	B	L	G
I	P	S	T	A	H	O	Z	A	R	F	C	Q	B	S	E	L	S
A	E	F	T	X	N	J	R	E	Z	L	H	N	J	L	Y	A	L
L	P	I	L	H	J	O	P	O	Y	K	E	S	L	A	S	H	L
S	B	S	L	T	G	O	R	Q	U	P	S	Z	K	U	G	N	A
E	A	S	O	W	Q	I	J	R	P	R	T	W	G	T	W	O	H
G	Z	L	C	Q	V	B	R	C	O	Q	R	A	U	I	Z	I	E
R	N	Z	P	W	K	S	O	L	L	O	A	O	C	R	A	T	I
E	L	C	C	I	N	S	S	R	I	A	S	L	S	I	X	U	G
G	L	S	O	T	B	H	E	N	N	V	D	E	Z	P	P	T	E
A	I	Y	I	M	K	P	X	R	X	J	I	W	V	S	K	I	N
T	L	T	M	Q	D	Q	W	B	C	G	Q	C	S	E	K	T	R
I	L	N	P	L	W	Q	O	Y	K	J	B	H	J	G	L	S	A
O	L	F	A	H	B	P	R	Y	M	M	A	R	G	M	F	N	C
N	L	O	A	J	L	F	X	M	O	R	Q	U	D	B	X	O	T
B	E	E	U	R	O	P	E	A	N	T	O	U	R	S	K	C	Y

Find These Words

ELEANORROOSEVEL   OPERA   GRAMMY

RACIALSEGREGATION   SPIRITUALS   CIVILRIGHTS

ORCHESTRAS   EUROPEANTOURS   CONSTITUTIONHALL

CARNEGIEHALL

Directions: Read and answer the questions. These are your opinions so the answers will vary.

How has music evolved over time and why is it important to our culture?

Who is your favorite musician and why?

What kind of music do you like to listen to?

Directions: Read and answer the questions below. There are clues in the puzzle to help you. Try and solve the cryptic message.

Clue for cryptic message: Marian's voice.

Questions

1) In one year, Marian _____ 26,000 miles in the longest tour in concert history, giving 70 concerts in five months.

2) The conductor _____ Toscanini reportedly told Marian she had "a voice heard but once in a century."

3) Albert _____, was very anti-discrimination, hosted Marian on many occasions, the first being in 1937 when she was denied a hotel room while performing at Princeton University.

4) Marian Anderson sang at President John F Kennedy's _____.

5) Marian was the first African American to sing with New York's Metropolitan _____.

6) President Eisenhower appointed Marian a delegate to the 13th General Assembly of the United _____.

7) Marian was given the Grammy Award for _____ Achievement.

8) Marian was the first African American singer to perform at the _____ House.

9) On Easter Sunday 1939 Marian performed on the steps of the _____ Memorial in Washington, D.C. to a crowd of 75,000 people that contained both blacks and whites helping start the civil rights movement for equality.

193

Directions: This is the WGLT Challenge. Solve the cryptogram. As the puzzle solver, you need to find which number belongs to which character. And this can be pretty challenging! You will need to match the number with the letter. There are some letters given to you below. This will help you solve the other words and unlock more characters. **Good Luck.**

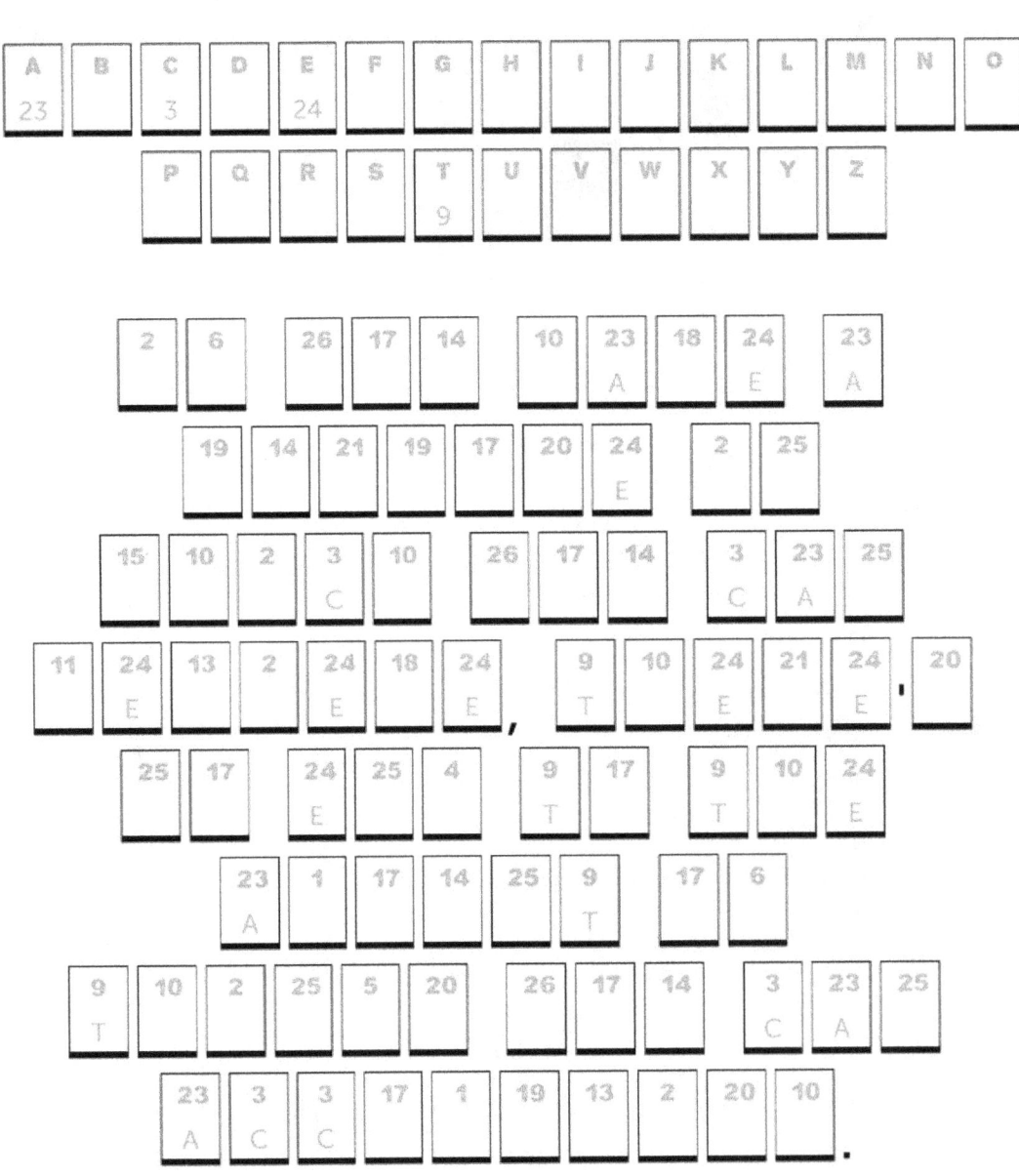

Robyn Fenty

Robyn Fenty

FEBRUARY 20, 1988 - PRESENT
BARBADIAN SINGER

LEFT BLANK ON PURPOSE

Robyn Fenty

Robyn Fenty

Robyn Fenty

Robyn Fenty

Robyn Fenty

Robyn Fenty

Directions: read the bio below and answer the following questions.

Hi, my name is Robyn Rihanna Fenty. I was born on February 20, 1988, in Saint Michael, Barbados. When I was 11, I was an army cadet in a sub-military program. When I was around 15, I formed a musical trio with some of my classmates. A record producer from America by the name of Evan Rogers discovered me. We recorded "Pon de Replay" and "The Last Time" for a demo tape. The demo was sent to Def Jam Recordings. Jay Z heard it and brought me in and the next thing I knew, we were signing a six-album deal. In 2005, I released my debut album, Music of the Sun and my first single was "Pon de Replay." In early 2006, I released my second studio album, A Girl like Me. In late 2006, I also made my acting debut in a cameo role in the film Bring It On: All or Nothing. Some of the songs that I'm known for are "Umbrella," "Rude Boy," "Don't Stop the Music," and "What's My Name."

1. How old was I when I got discovered?
    A. 14
    B. 17
    C. 15
2. What year did I release my first album?
    A. 2005
    B. 2006
    C. 2003
3. What is the name of the record label that signed me?
    A. Arista Records
    B. Def Jam Records
    C. Priority Records

Directions: Answer the questions, to solve the crossword puzzle. You can use the internet if you get stuck on any question.

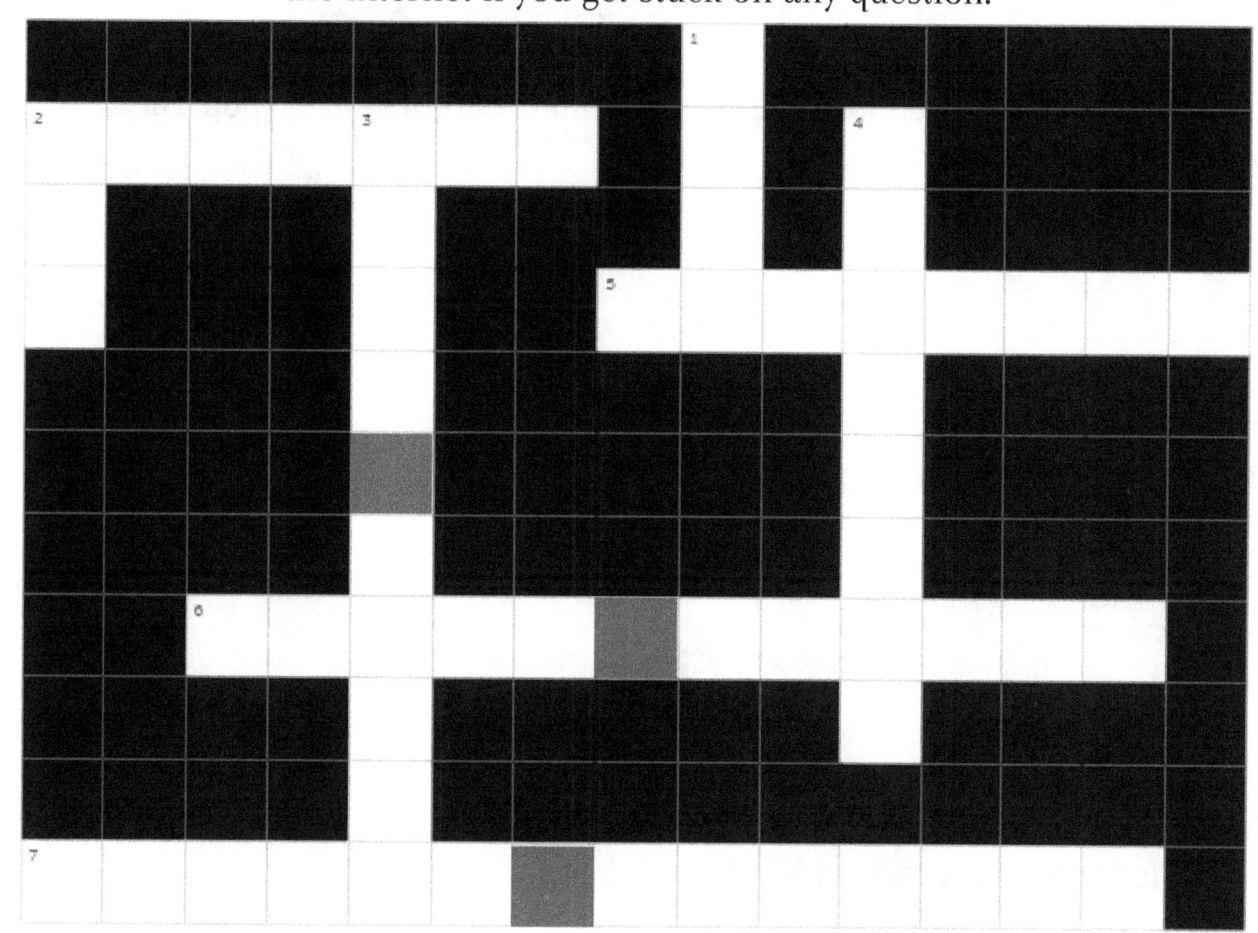

Across
2) Rihanna is a mezzo-_____, with a range spanning from B2 to C♯6.
5) Rihanna has a day named after her in Barbados, which is _____ 22nd.
6) Rihanna founded the _____ Foundation (CLF) in 2012, in honor of her grandparents.
7) Rihanna won the title of 'Miss Combermere', in her high school's _____.

Down
1) Rihanna was the first woman to win '_____ of the Year' award.
2) Rihanna's been in the Guinness World Book of Records ___ times.
3) Rihanna was an _____ in a sub-military programme.
4) Rihanna was declared a National Hero of _____ on the first day of the country's parliamentary republic in 2021.

Directions: Read and answer the questions. These are your opinions so the answers will vary.

Can you name some famous musicians from different genres (pop, rock, classical, jazz, etc.)?

What instruments can you name?

What is your favorite song and who is it by?

Directions: Unscramble the words below about Robyn. See if you can get the bonus word.

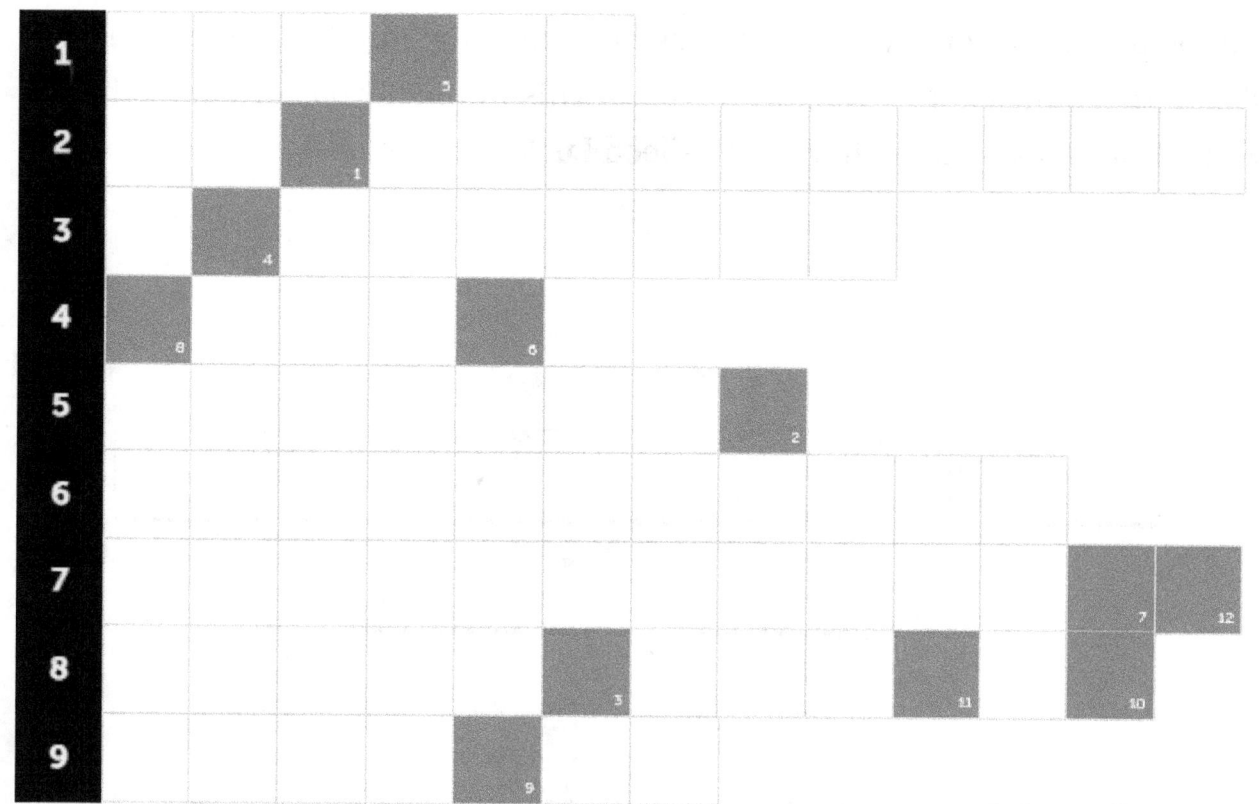

BONUS WORD

1	2	3	4	5	6

7	8	9	10	11	12

Unscramble Words

1) eigrsn
2) ueoinnswssbma
3) ibnabadar
4) beofsr
5) baelulmr
6) mrwgdaaarym
7) alysugxmnaasg
8) svluounitoti
9) acrtses

201

Directions: This is the WGLT Challenge. Solve the cryptogram. As the puzzle solver, you need to find which number belongs to which character. And this can be pretty challenging! You will need to match the number with the letter. There are some letters given to you below. This will help you solve the other words and unlock more characters. **Good Luck.**

Aretha Franklin
Answers

1. How old was I when I signed with J.V.B. Records?
   - A. 16
   - B. 12
   - C. 14
2. What year did I sign with Atlantic Records?
   - A. 1966
   - B. 1960
   - C. 1968
3. I was the first female performer to what?
   - A. Get inducted into the Musicians Hall of Fame
   - B. Get inducted into the Rock and Roll Hall of Fame
   - C. Get inducted into America's Pop Music Hall of Fame

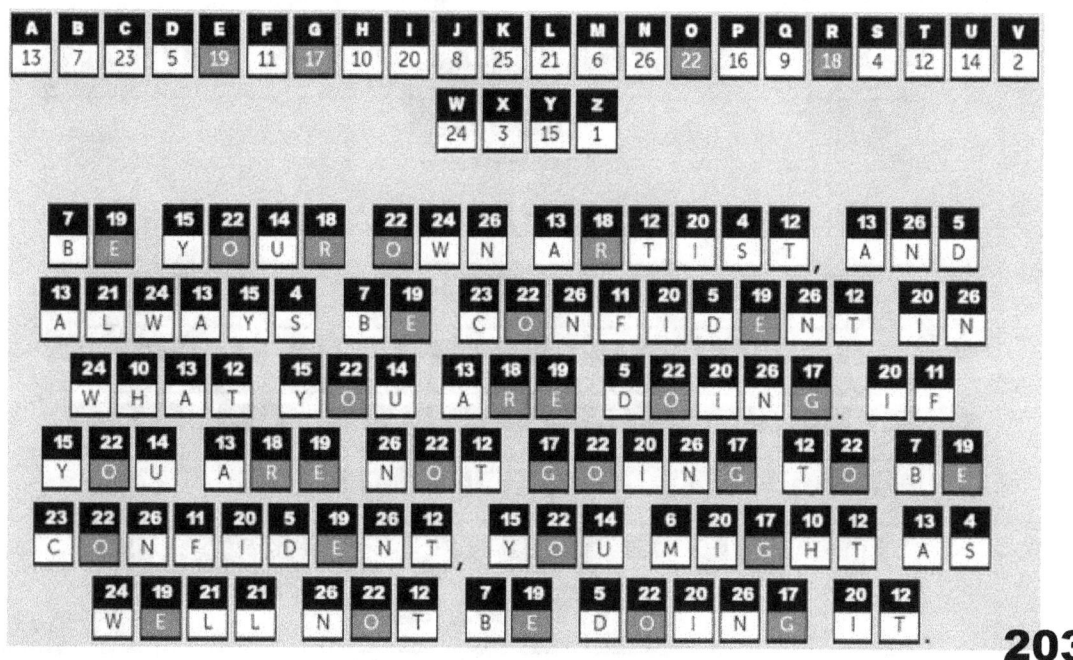

"BE YOUR OWN ARTIST, AND ALWAYS BE CONFIDENT IN WHAT YOU ARE DOING. IF YOU ARE NOT GOING TO BE CONFIDENT, YOU MIGHT AS WELL NOT BE DOING IT."

203

1. How did I learn to play the trumpet?
   A. Music teacher
   B. Church
   C. By ear
2. What nickname stuck with me thru the years?
   A. Dippermouth
   B. Satchmo
   C. Satchelmouth
3. What city is in my heart every time I play the trumpet?
   A. Chicago
   B. Jacksonville
   C. New Orleans

Louis Armstrong Answers

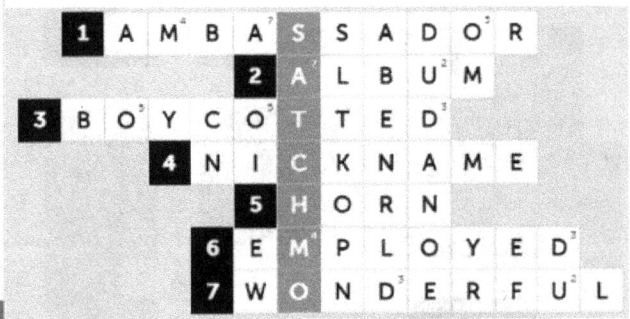

1. AMBASSADOR
2. ALBUM
3. BOYCOTTED
4. NICKNAME
5. HORN
6. EMPLOYED
7. WONDERFUL

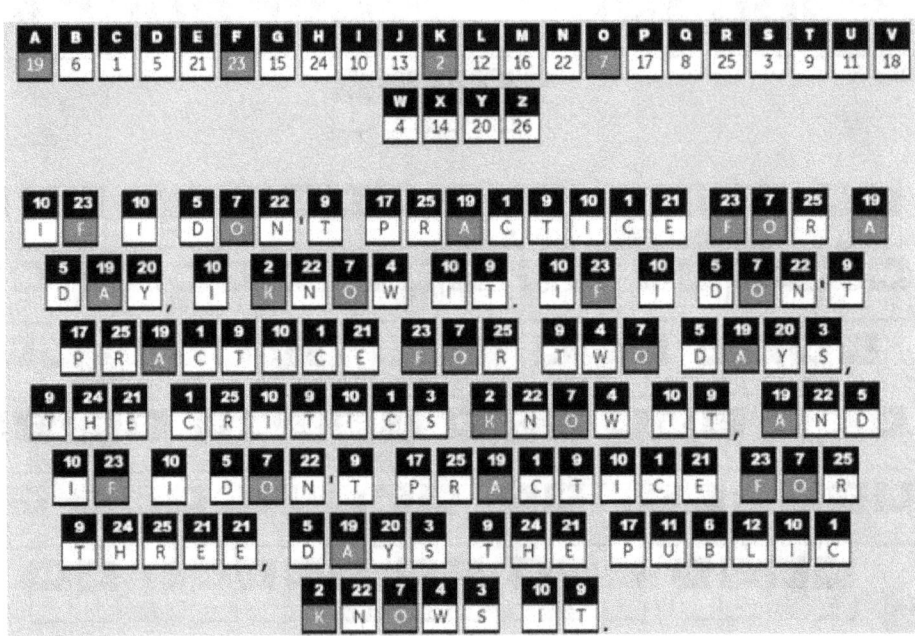

IF I DON'T PRACTICE FOR A DAY, I KNOW IT. IF I DON'T PRACTICE FOR TWO DAYS, THE CRITICS KNOW IT, AND IF I DON'T PRACTICE FOR THREE, DAYS THE PUBLIC KNOWS IT.

204

1. Who did I perform with when I was younger?
   A. Gladys Knight
   B. Michael Jackson
   C. Whitney Houston
2. How old was I when I signed my first record deal?
   A. 14
   B. 13
   C. 12
3. My first film I was in was?
   A. Queen of the Damned
   B. Romeo Must Die
   C. New York Undercover

Aaliyah Haughton
Answers

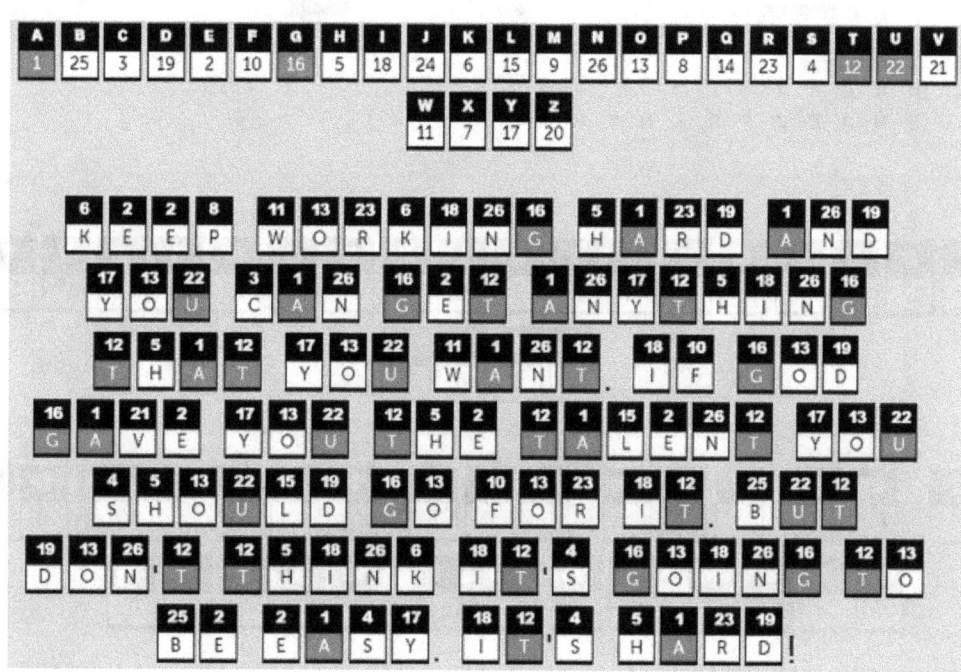

KEEP WORKING HARD AND YOU CAN GET ANYTHING THAT YOU WANT. IF GOD GAVE YOU THE TALENT YOU SHOULD GO FOR IT. BUT DON'T THINK IT'S GOING TO BE EASY. IT'S HARD!

205

John Gillespie
Answers

1. **What instrument was I known for playing?**
   A. Piano
   B. Trumpet
   C. Trombone
2. **What year did I run for President?**
   A. 1960
   B. 1968
   C. 1964
3. **I was known as who during the State Department tour?**
   A. Dizzy
   B. Mr. Gillespie
   C. Ambassador of Jazz

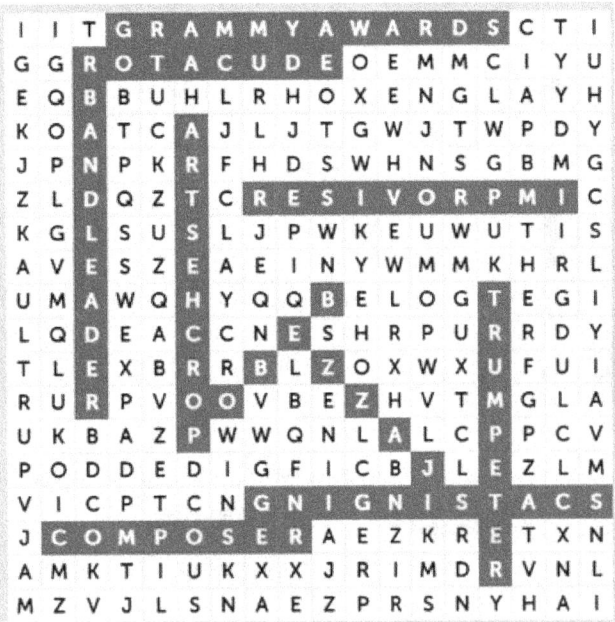

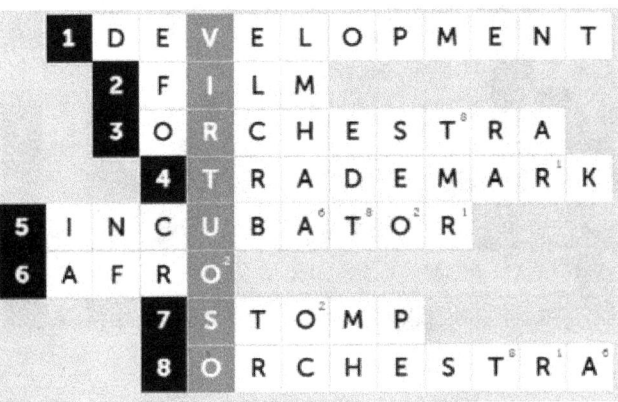

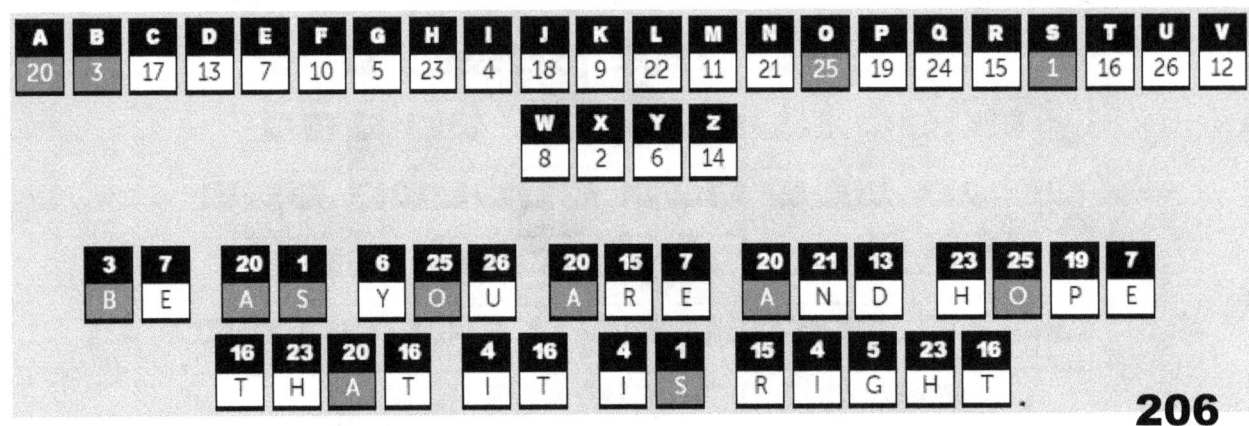

206

1. Where did I debut my hit song Strange Fruit?
   A. Carnegie Hall
   B. Cafe Society
   C. Cotton Club
2. How old was I when I started singing in night clubs?
   A. 18
   B. 15
   C. 14
3. I was the first African American woman to what?
   A. Perform with a white singer
   B. Perform with a white orchestra
   C. Perform with a white pianist

Eleanora Fagan

Answers

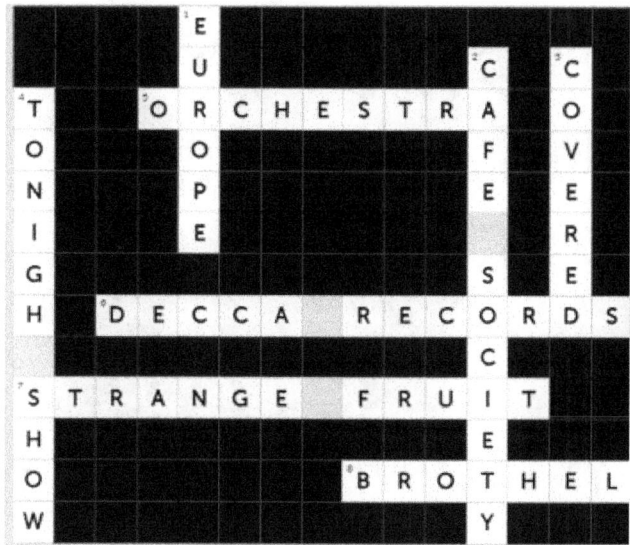

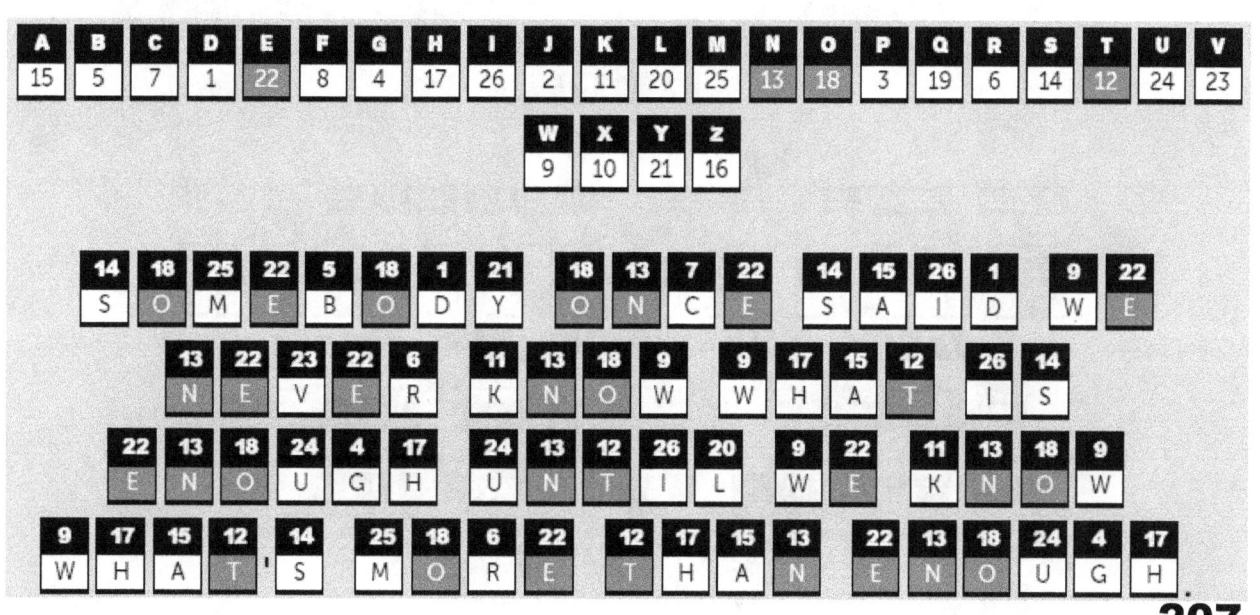

SOMEBODY ONCE SAID WE NEVER KNOW WHAT IS ENOUGH UNTIL WE KNOW WHAT'S MORE THAN ENOUGH

207

Michael Jackson Answers

1. What did the Jackson 5 do at the Apollo Theater?
   A. Win
   B. Lose
   C. Didn't get to perform
2. What year did the Jackson 5 get introduced?
   A. 1968
   B. 1969
   C. 1967
3. Jackson 5 first TV appearance was on what show?
   A. Ed Sullivan Show
   B. American Band Stand
   C. Miss Black America pageant

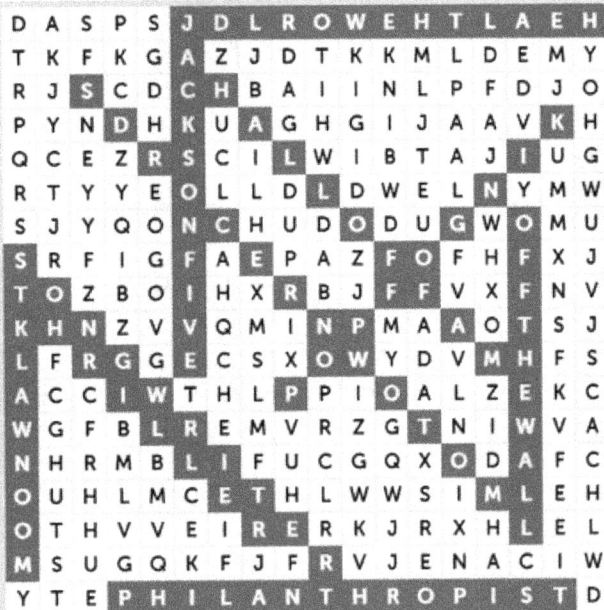

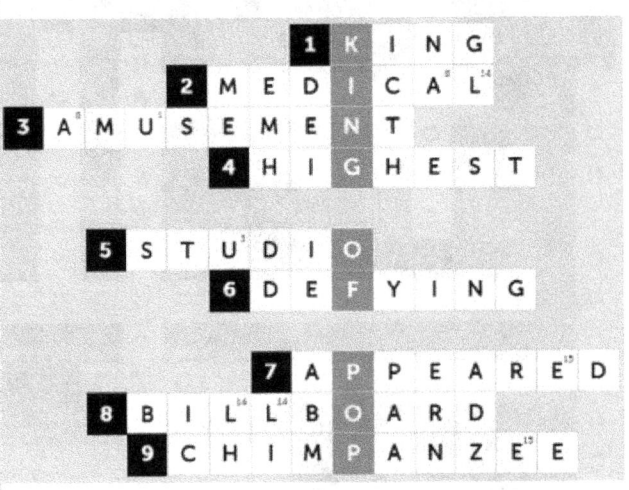

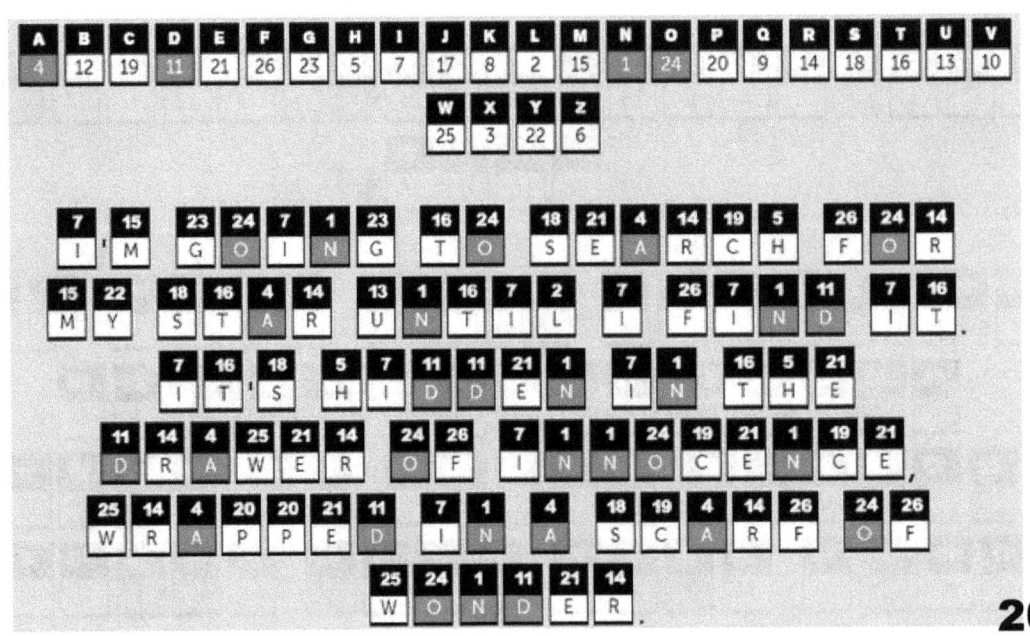

I'M GOING TO SEARCH FOR MY STAR UNTIL I FIND IT. IT'S HIDDEN IN THE DRAWER OF INNOCENCE, WRAPPED IN A SCARF OF WONDER.

208

1. What age did I start playing the piano?
   A. 5
   B. 4
   C. 6
2. What school did I want to get accepted to?
   A. Juilliard School
   B. Curtis Institute of Music
   C. Allen High School for girls
3. I changed my stage name while performing here?
   A. Greenwich Village
   B. Ronnie Scott's Jazz Club
   C. Midtown Bar & Grill

Eunice Waymon

Answers

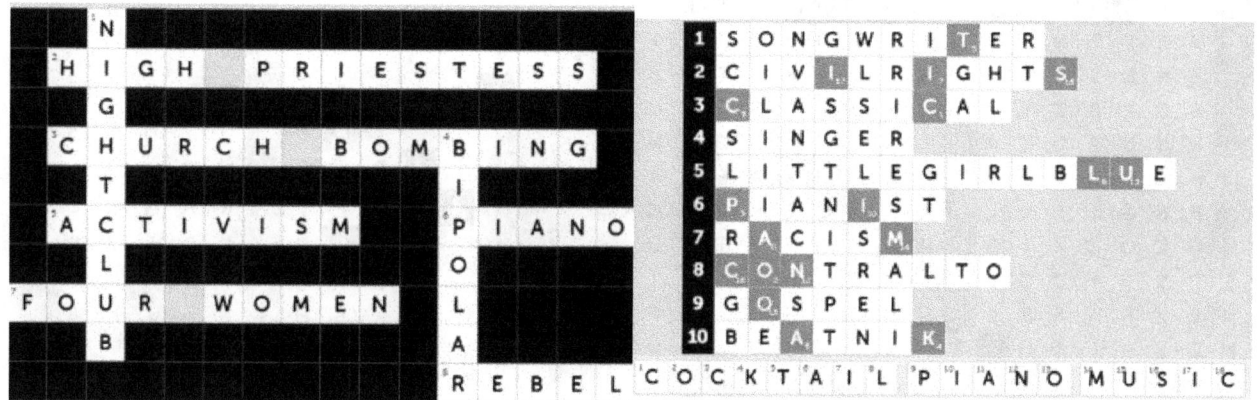

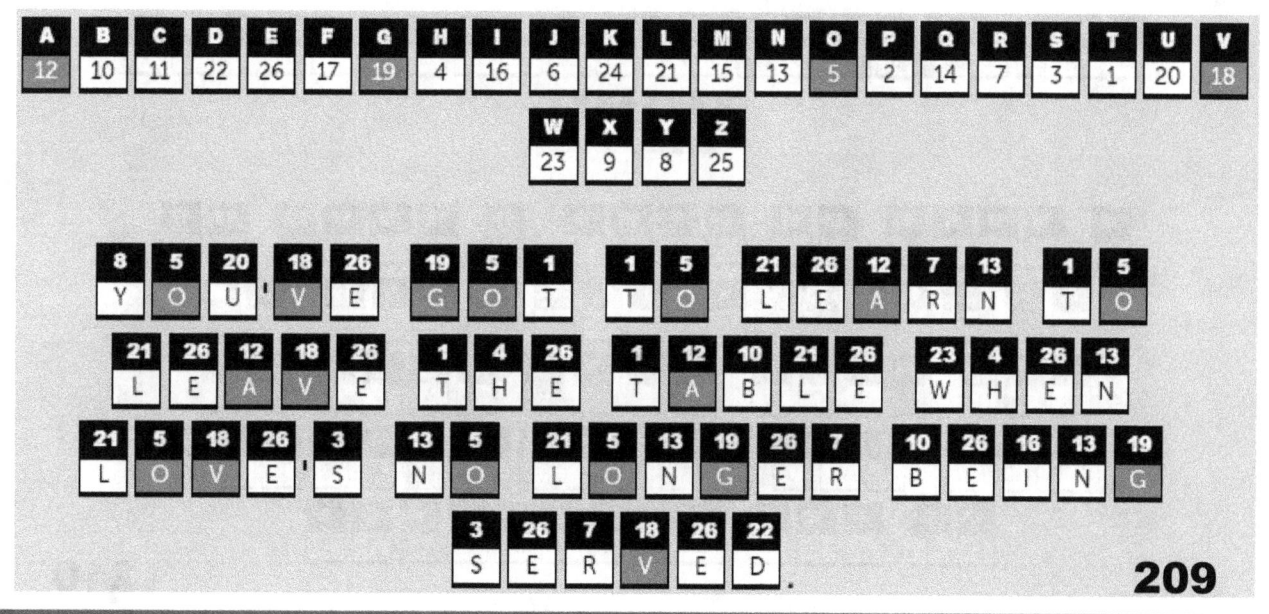

"YOU'VE GOT TO LEARN TO LEAVE THE TABLE WHEN LOVE'S NO LONGER BEING SERVED."

209

1. What did I start my career off doing?
   A. Playing the piano
   B. Backup Dancer
   C. Doing Theater
2. What year did I release arguably my best album?
   A. 1993
   B. 1991
   C. 1995
3. Which song was my come out song in the industry?
   A. Same Song
   B. Dear Mama
   C. Me Against the World

Lesane Parish Crooks

Answers

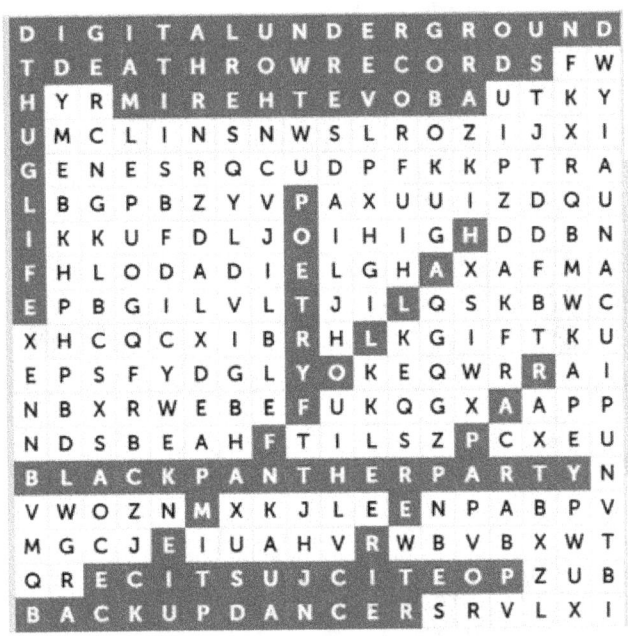

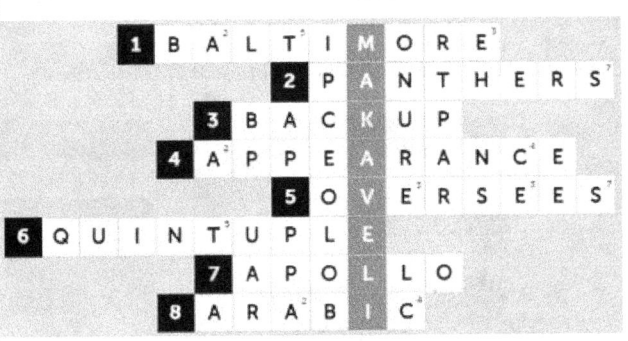

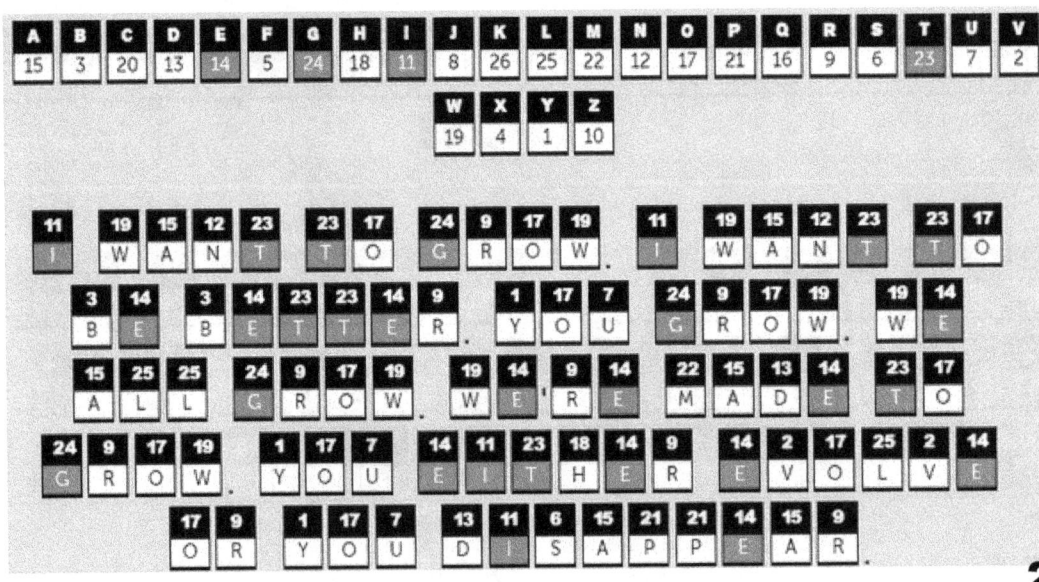

I WANT TO GROW. I WANT TO
BE BETTER. YOU GROW. WE
ALL GROW. WE'RE MADE TO
GROW. YOU EITHER EVOLVE
OR YOU DISAPPEAR.

210

1. What was my first hit song?
   A. You Give Good Love
   B. Hold Me
   C. I Will Always Love You
2. I set a record with how many consecutive #1 hits?
   A. 8
   B. 6
   C. 7
3. I have a Guinness World Record for what?
   A. Most Diamond Singles
   B. Most awarded female act
   C. Most singles sold

Whitney Houston
Answers

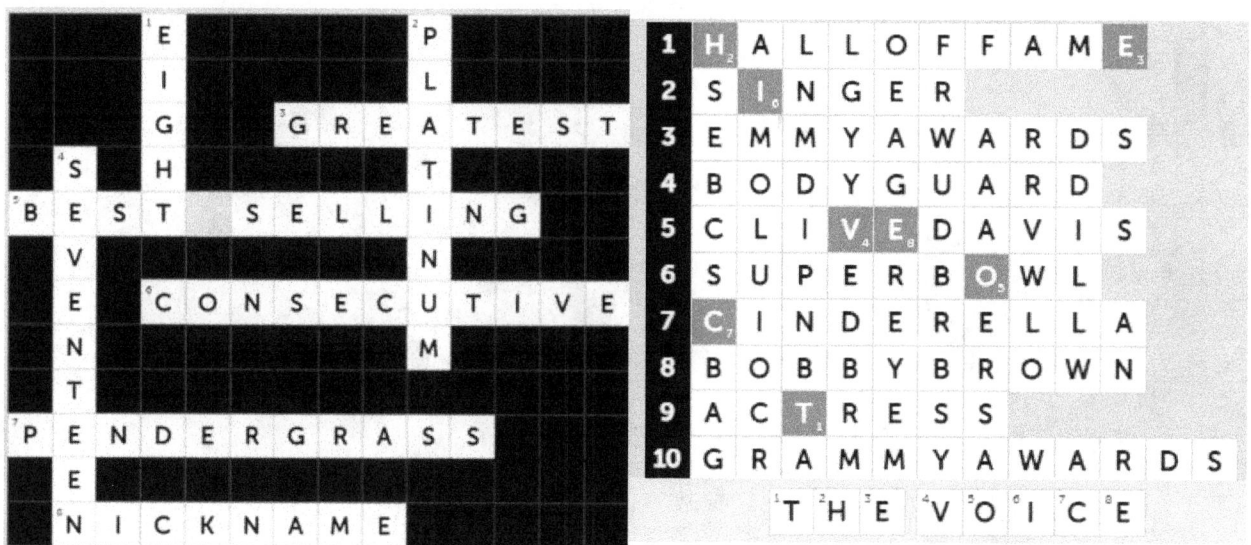

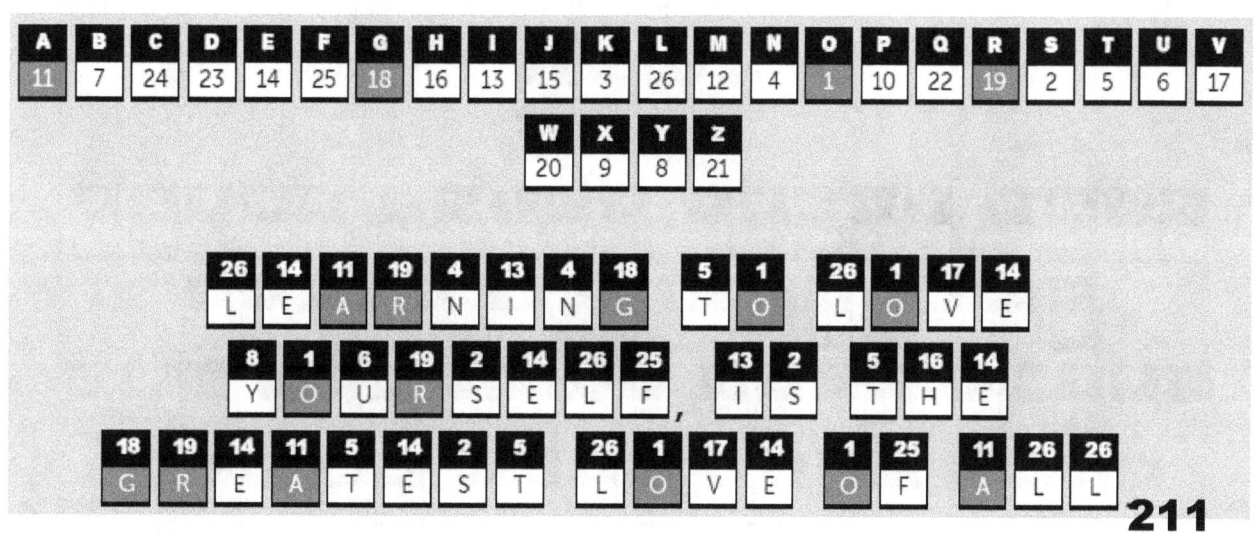

LEARNING TO LOVE YOURSELF, IS THE GREATEST LOVE OF ALL

211

O'Shea Jackson
Answers

1. How old was I when I sold my first song?
   A. 21
   B. 16
   C. 14
2. What album was rap's first EP certified Platinum?
   A. Kill At Will
   B. AmeriKKKA's Most Wanted
   C. Predator
3. What is my degree in?
   A. Computers
   B. Education
   C. Architectural Drafting

1. FIRST
2. DIRECTOR
3. ACTION
4. NAMED
5. GANGSTA
6. BOYZ

A	B	C	D	E	F	G	H	I	J	K	L	M	N	O	P	Q	R	S	T	U	V
16	23	22	11	26	7	6	10	21	9	20	19	13	1	24	4	14	5	25	8	15	17	18

W	X	Y	Z
3	12	6	2

DON'T WORRY ABOUT BEING A STAR. WORRY ABOUT DOING GOOD WORK AND ALL THAT WILL COME TO YOU

.212

1. What got me started in my singing career?
   A. I was notice in a Night Club
   B. Winning Amateur Nights at the Apollo Theater
   C. My Church
2. What was my biggest song?
   A. A-Tisket, A-Tasket
   B. Love and Kisses
   C. It Don't Mean a Thing (If It Ain't Got That Swing)
3. I was the first African American woman to?
   A. Have a Platinum song
   B. Perform at the Super Bowl
   C. Win a Grammy Award

Ella Fitzgerald
Answers

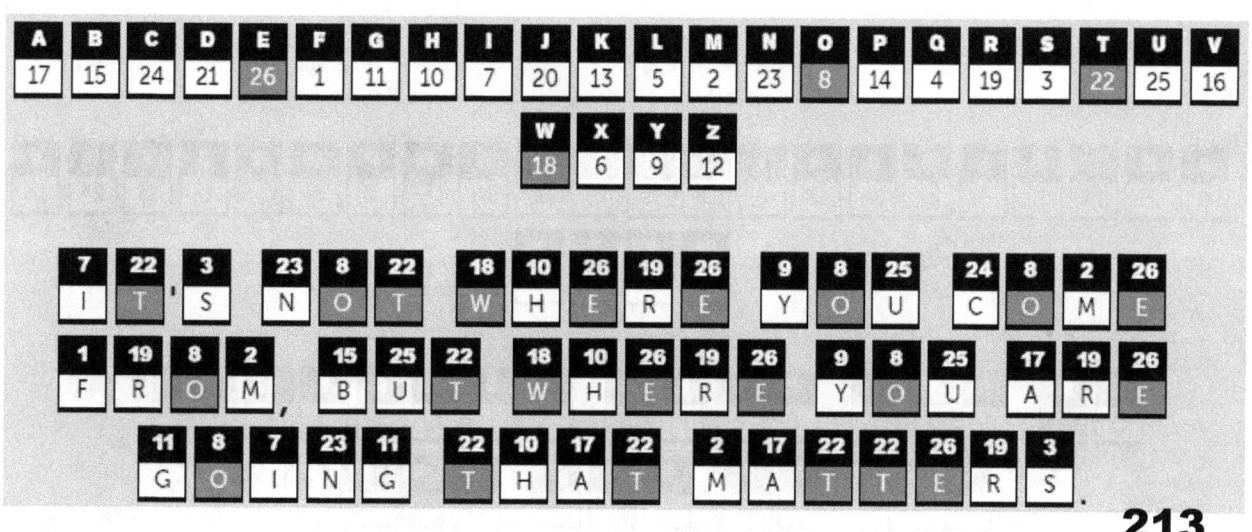

"IT'S NOT WHERE YOU COME FROM, BUT WHERE YOU ARE GOING THAT MATTERS."

213

1. What school did I go to for music theory?
   A. Juilliard School
   B. East St. Louis Lincoln High School
   C. Manhattan School of Music
2. What year did Cool Jazz begin?
   A. 1948
   B. 1957
   C. 1953
3. I dropped out of Institute of Musical Arts to focus on?
   A. Music
   B. Dancing
   C. Theater

Miles Dewey Davis III
Answers

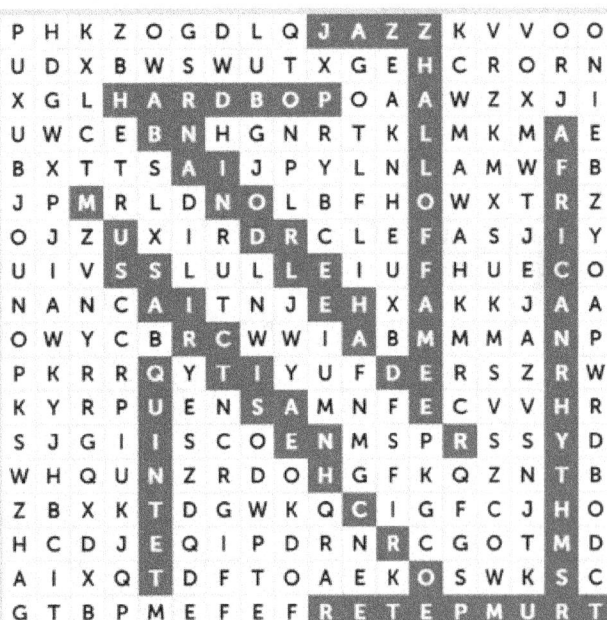

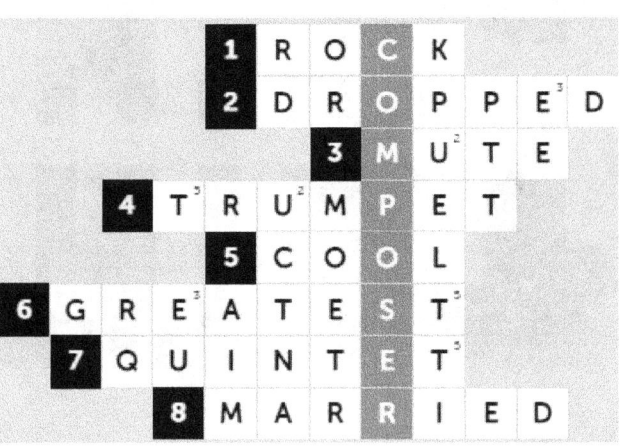

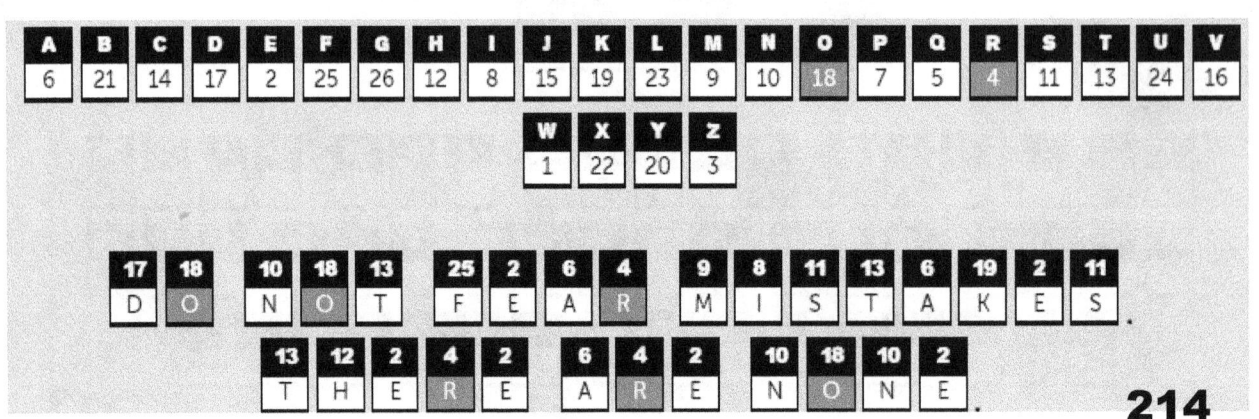

DO NOT FEAR MISTAKES.
THERE ARE NONE.

214

Diana Ross Answers

1. What got me an audition with Motown Records?
   A. A&R Rep
   B. Won talent contest
   C. Family
2. What year did I start my solo career?
   A. 1960
   B. 1972
   C. 1970
3. I was the first African American woman to what?
   A. Go Diamond
   B. Co-host the Academy Awards
   C. Co-host the NAACP Awards

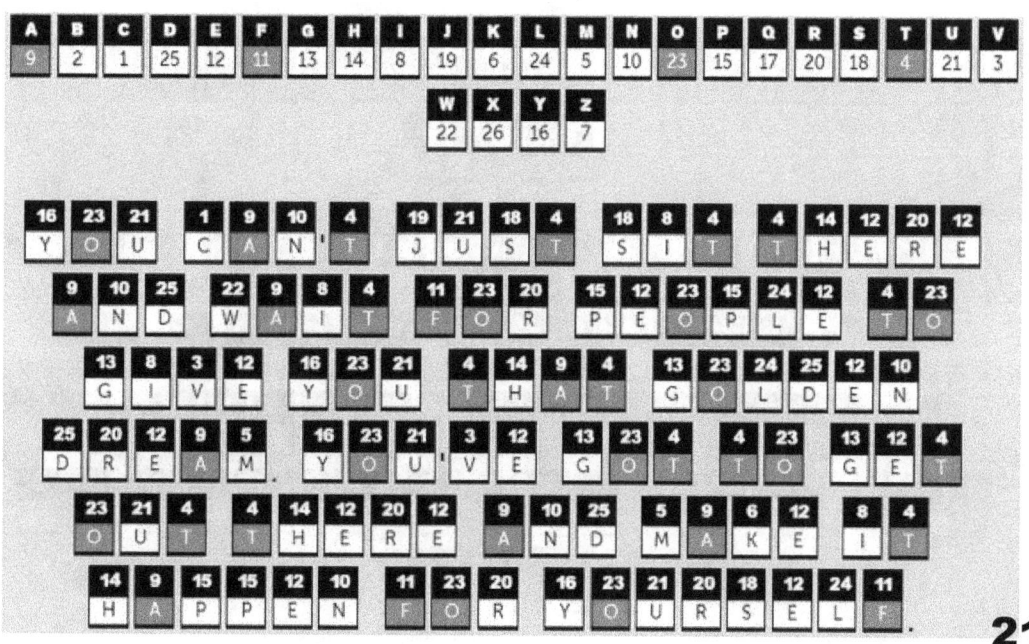

"You can't just sit there and wait for people to give you that golden dream. You've got to get out there and make it happen for yourself."

215

Shawn Carter Answers

1. Who didn't I go to High School with?
   A. Kanye West
   B. Notorious B.I.G.
   C. Busta Rhymes
2. What year did I help found Roc-A-Fella Records?
   A. 1999
   B. 1996
   C. 1995
3. I was the first solo rapper to do what?
   A. Go Diamond
   B. Be a millionaire
   C. Be inducted in the Rock and Roll Hall of Fame

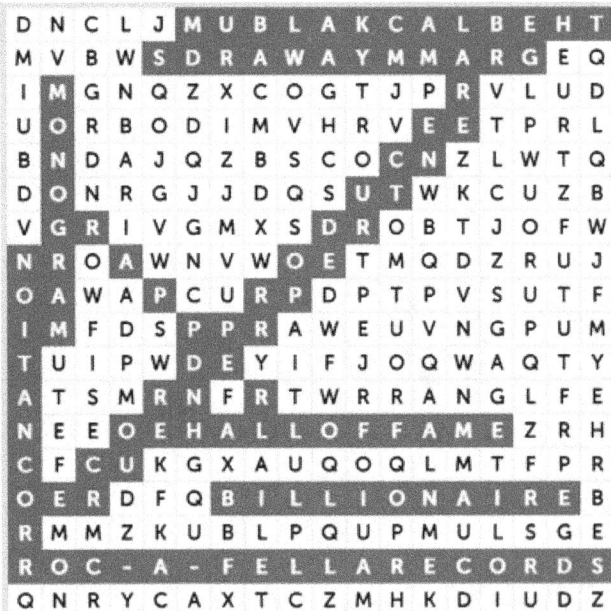

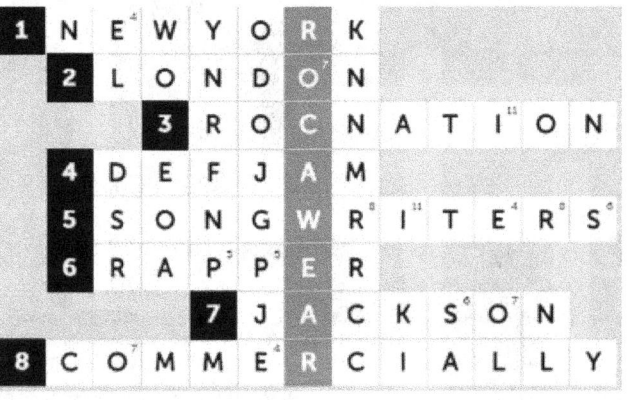

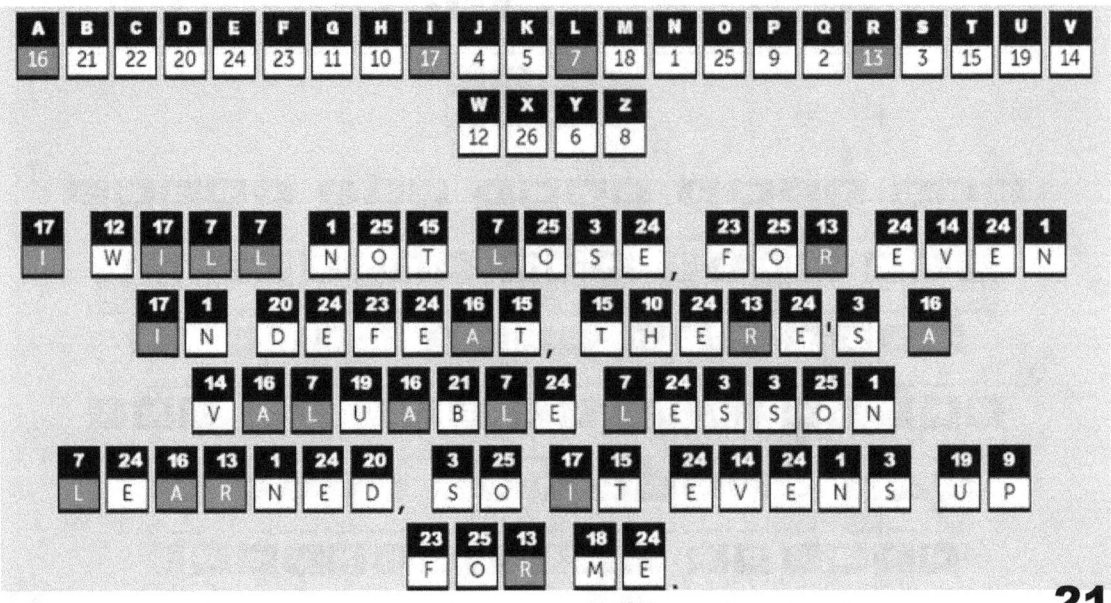

"I WILL NOT LOSE, FOR EVEN IN DEFEAT, THERE'S A VALUABLE LESSON LEARNED, SO IT EVENS UP FOR ME."

216

Hazel Scott Answers

1. What music instrument was I able to play by age four?
   A. Trumpet
   B. Piano
   C. Guitar
2. How old was I when I started performing radio?
   A. 18
   B. 14
   C. 16
3. I was the first African American in the U.S. to what?
   A. Perform in movies
   B. Be a millionaire
   C. Have my own TV show

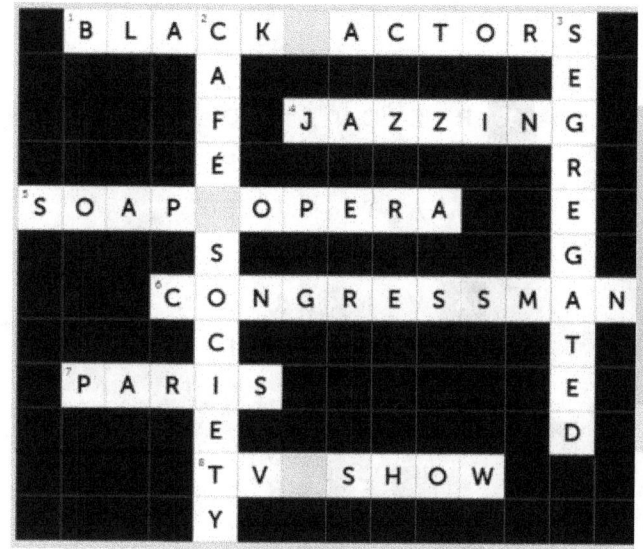

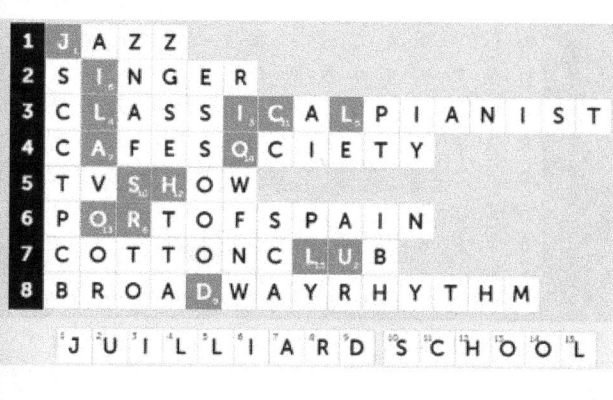

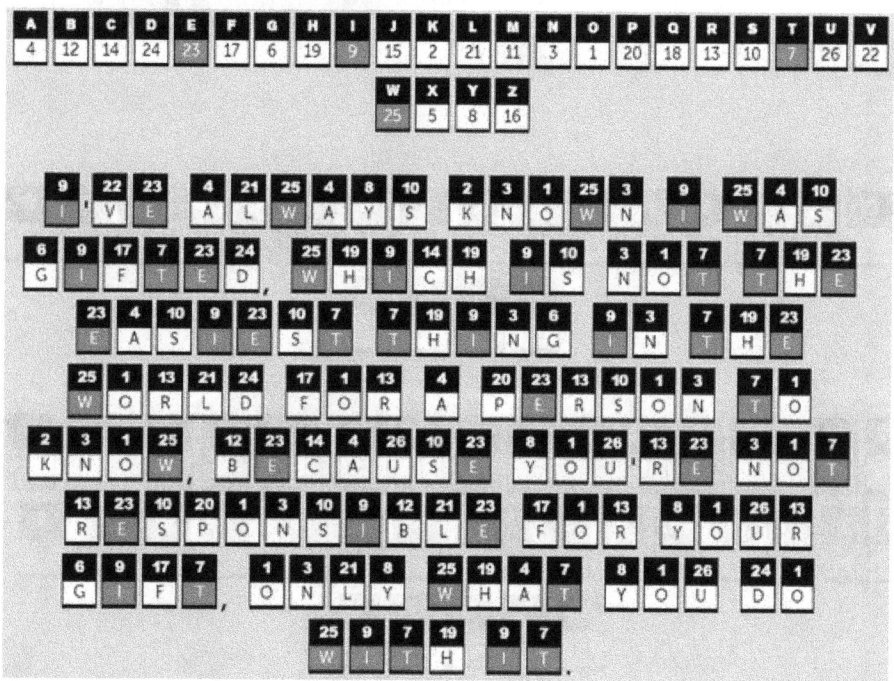

"I've always known I was gifted, which is not the easiest thing in the world for a person to know, because you're not responsible for your gift, only what you do with it."

217

Lawrence Parker
Answers

1. What year did I help found Boogie Down Productions?
   A. 1987
   B. 1986
   C. 1985
2. What movement did I start in response to violence?
   A. Stop the Violence Movement
   B. National Urban League
   C. NCAAP
3. I attracted many prominent emcees to appear on what?
   A. Tour
   B. Concert
   C. 12-inch single

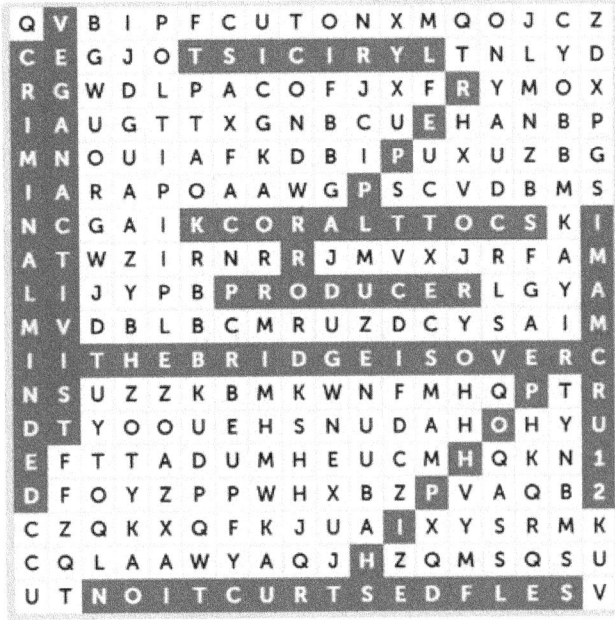

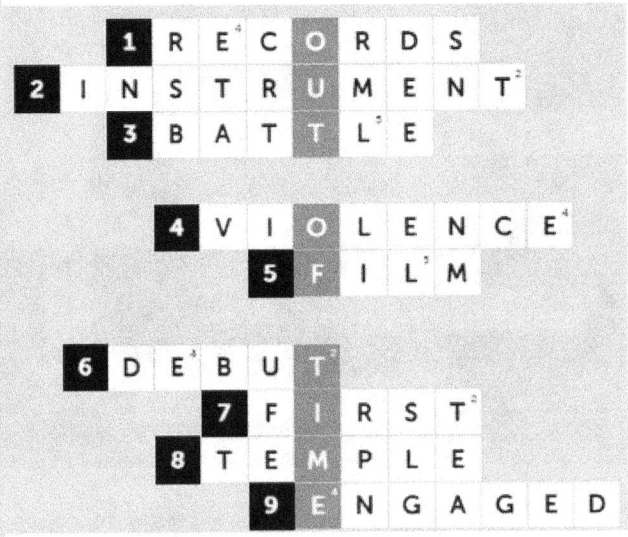

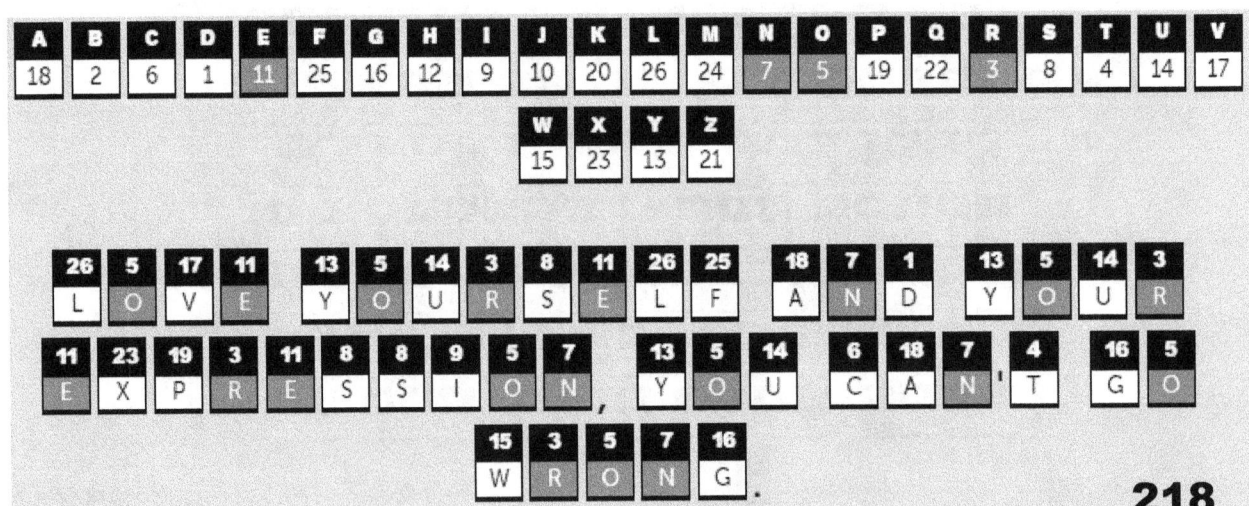

218

1. I was the first African American in the U.S. to what?
   A. To star in a TV series
   B. To star in a movie
   C. To star in a play
2. What year did I move to Harlem?
   A. 1920
   B. 1918
   C. 1919
3. How did I get my start in music business?
   A. I sang in a Nightclub
   B. Talent Search
   C. Won a singing competition

Ethel Waters

Answers

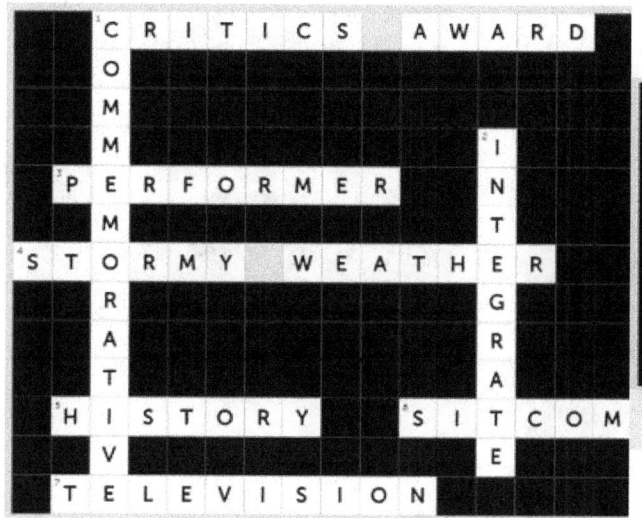

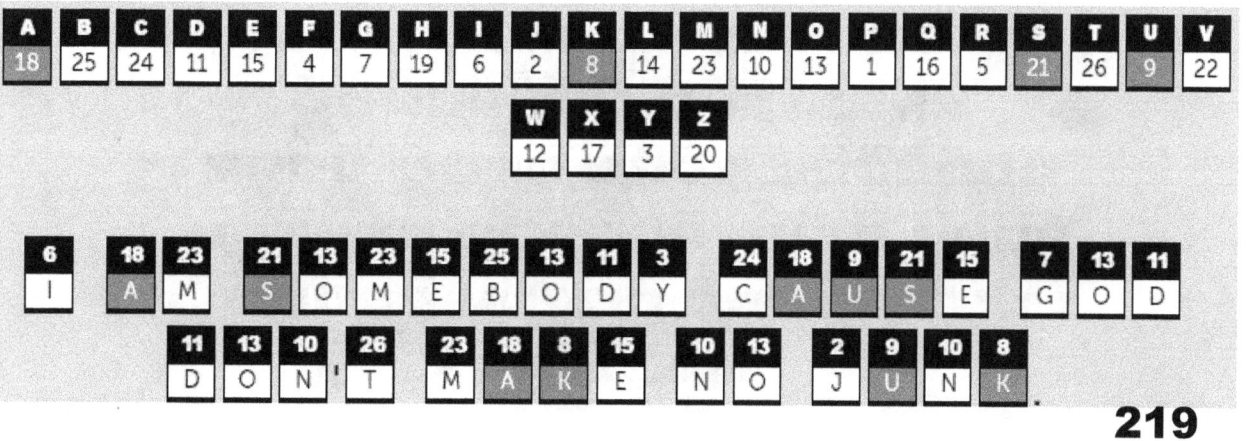

219

Willard Smith II
Answers

1. What song was my first big hit?
   A. Parents Just Don't Understand
   B. Summertime
   C. Girls Ain't Nothing but Trouble
2. What year did we sign with Jive Records?
   A. 1987
   B. 1986
   C. 1990
3. Our group was the first rap group to what?
   A. Sell 10 million records
   B. Win a Grammy Award for Best Rap Performance
   C. Win a Grammy Award for Best Rap Album

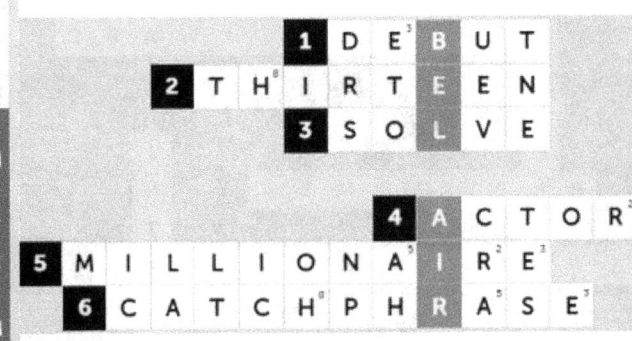

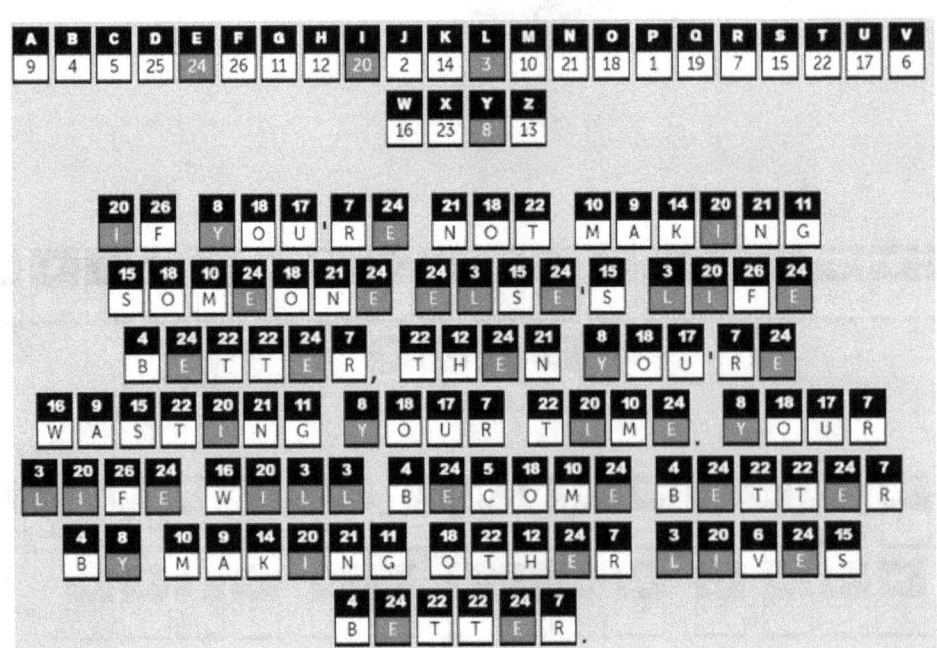

IF YOU'RE NOT MAKING SOMEONE ELSE'S LIFE BETTER, THEN YOU'RE WASTING YOUR TIME. YOUR LIFE WILL BECOME BETTER BY MAKING OTHER LIVES BETTER.

1. What was the name of the band I started with?
   A. Chapter 5
   B. Chapter 8
   C. Chapter 3
2. What song brought me my third Grammy win?
   A. Angel
   B. Sweet Love
   C. Ain't No Need to Worry
3. What record label released the album Rapture?
   A. Warner Music Group
   B. Ariola
   C. Beverly Glen Music

Anita Denise Baker
Answers

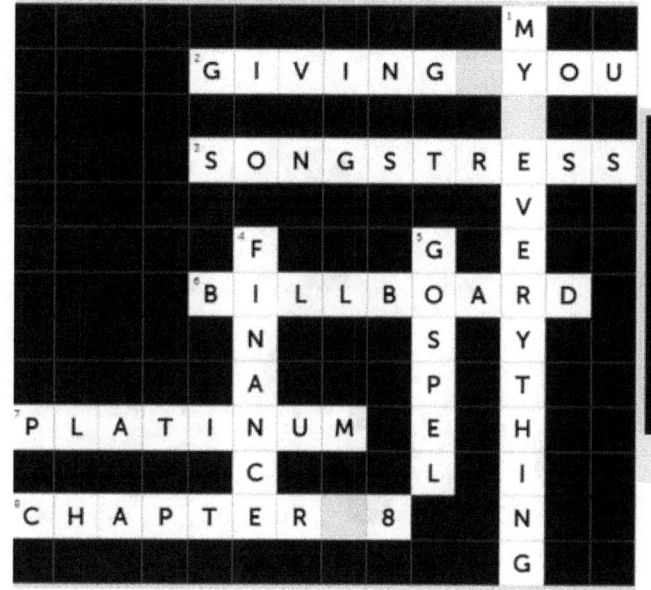

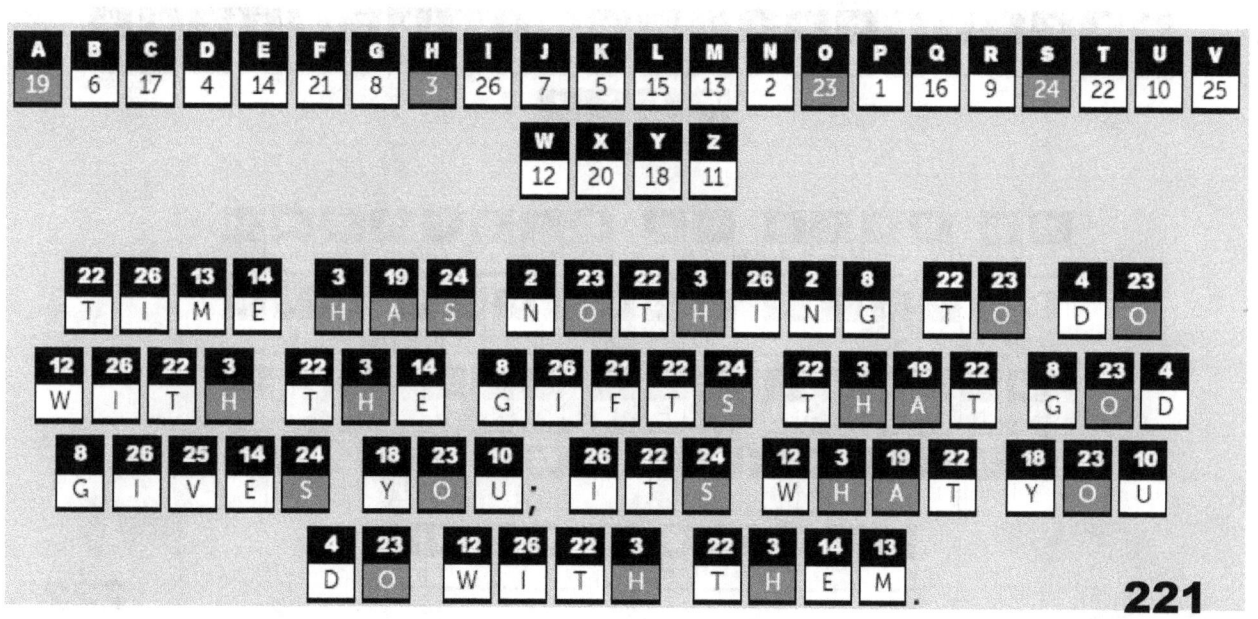

TIME HAS NOTHING TO DO WITH THE GIFTS THAT GOD GIVES YOU; IT'S WHAT YOU DO WITH THEM.

221

1. What was my first stage name?
   A. Nasty Nas
   B. Nas
   C. Kid Wave
2. What year did I drop arguably the best hip hop album?
   A. 1996
   B. 1994
   C. 1992
3. Which song is not one of mine?
   A. New York State of Mind
   B. If I Ruled the World
   C. Empire State of Mind

Nasir bin Olu Dara Jones

Answers

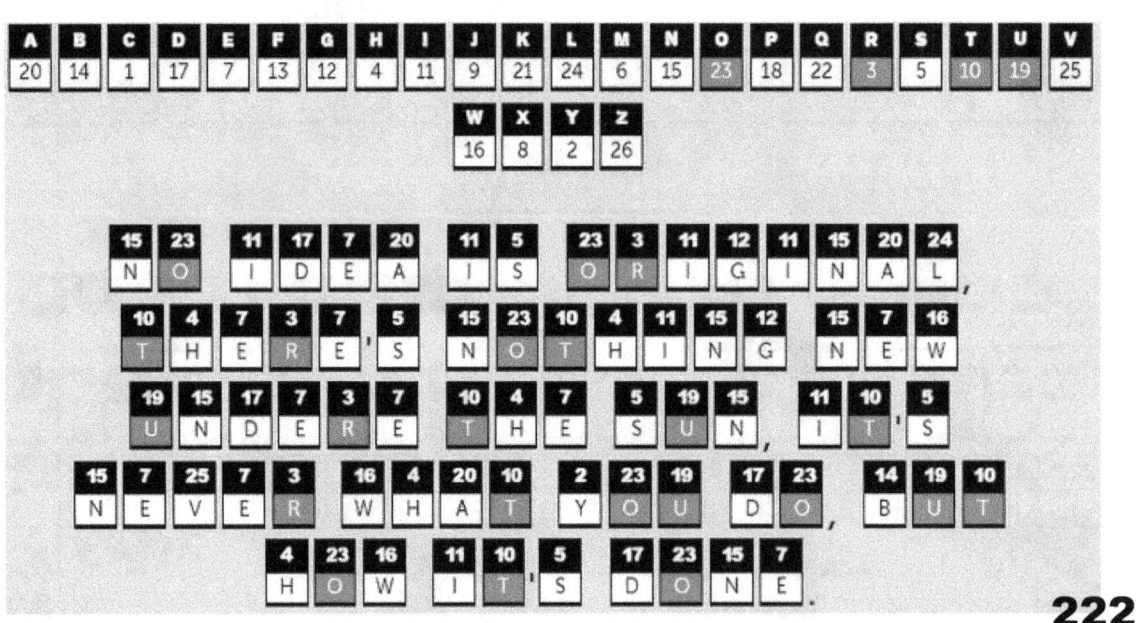

222

Pearl Mae Bailey Answers

1. What college did I graduate from?
   A. Temple University
   B. Georgetown University
   C. New York University
2. What year did I host The Pearl Bailey Show?
   A. 1971
   B. 1867
   C. 1974
3. I won amateur contest at what Theatre?
   A. Earle Theatre
   B. Mastbaum Theatre
   C. Pearl Theatre

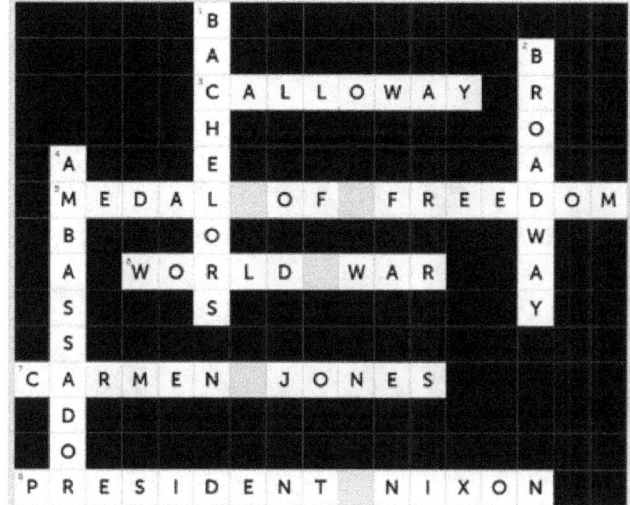

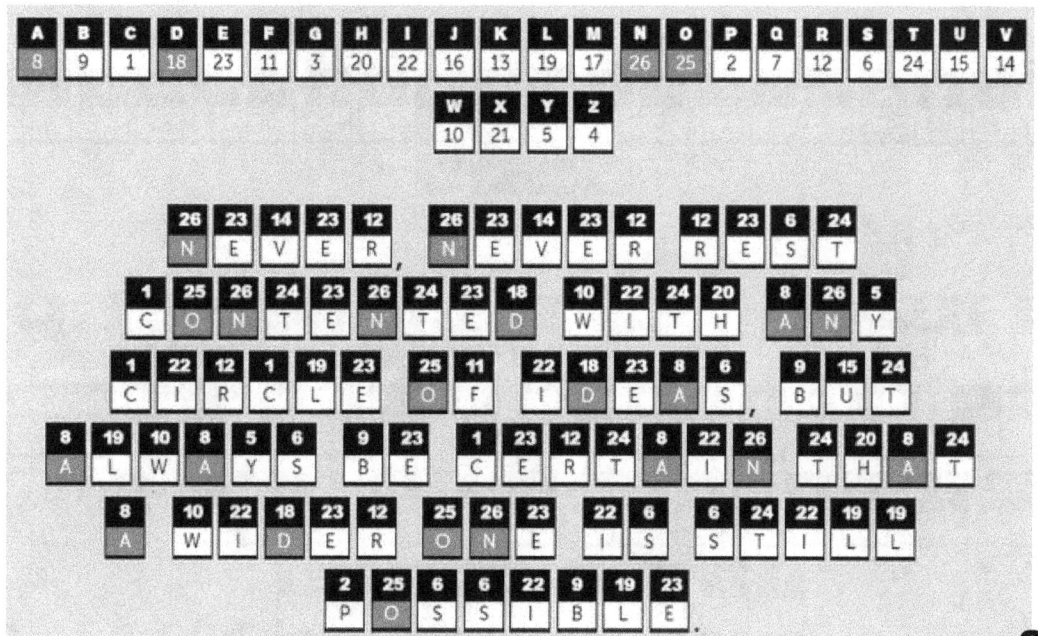

"Never, never rest contented with any circle of ideas, but always be certain that a wider one is still possible."

Beyoncé Knowles
Answers

1. What was the name of my group when I first started?
   A. Destiny's Child
   B. En Vogue
   C. Girl's Tyme

2. What year did I release my debut solo album?
   A. 1996
   B. 2003
   C. 2000

3. I was the first solo artist to do what?
   A. Have six studio albums debut at number one
   B. Have six studio albums go platinum
   C. Have six studio albums debut at number one overseas

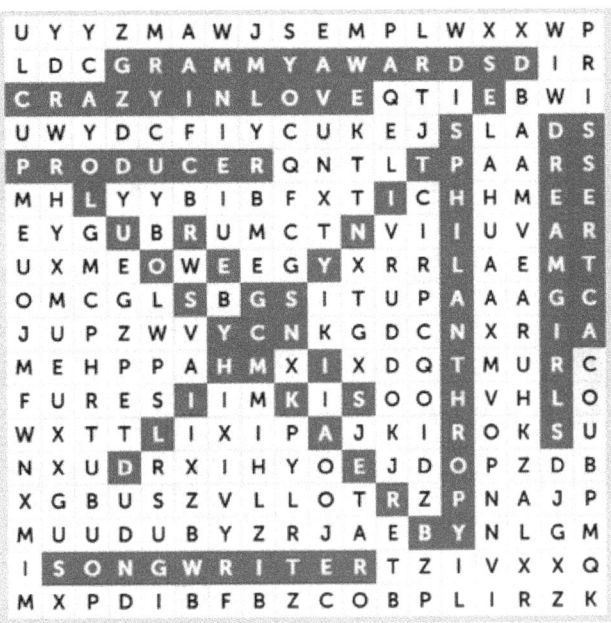

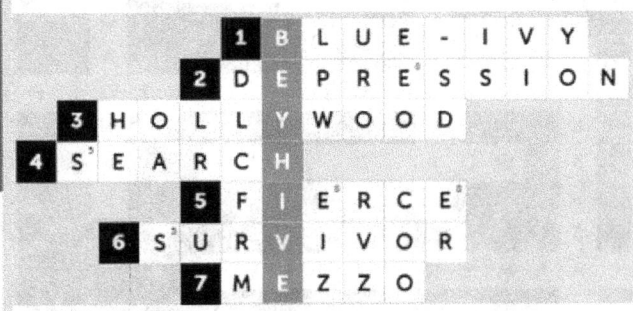

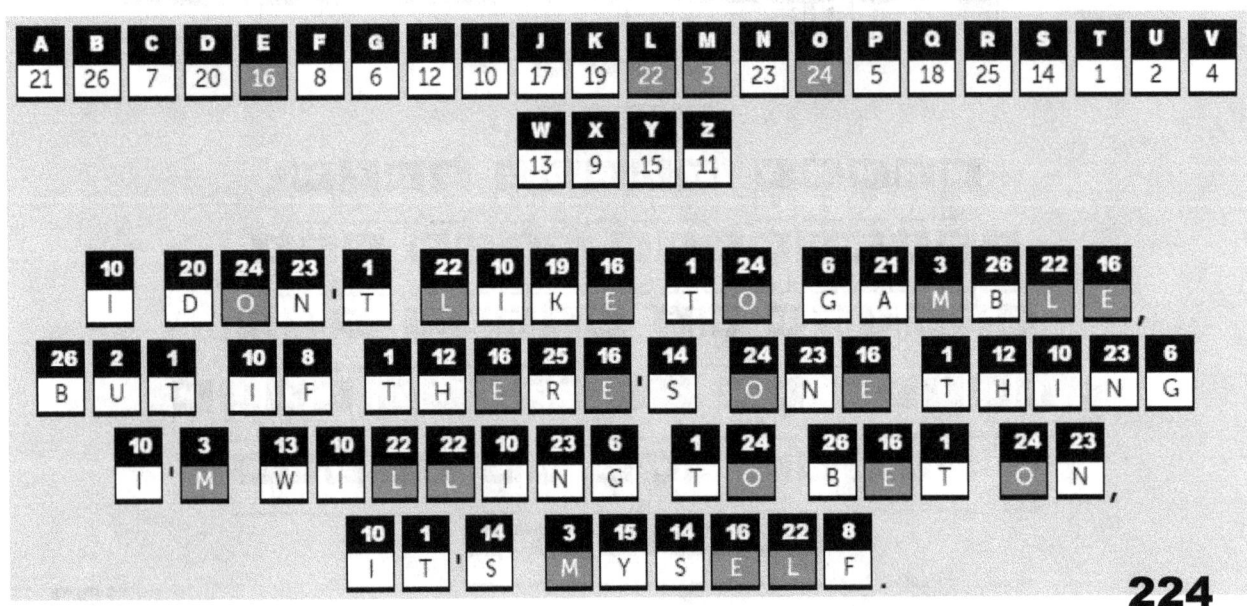

I DON'T LIKE TO GAMBLE, BUT IF THERE'S ONE THING I'M WILLING TO BET ON, IT'S MYSELF.

224

Zenzile Miriam Makeba
Answers

1. What age did they realize my gift with singing?
   A. 6
   B. 10
   C. 8
2. What year did I find a national reputation?
   A. 1953
   B. 1960
   C. 1956
3. I was the first South African to do what in the U.S.?
   A. Do a Broadway Play
   B. Make the Billboard Top 100
   C. Star in an U.S. movie

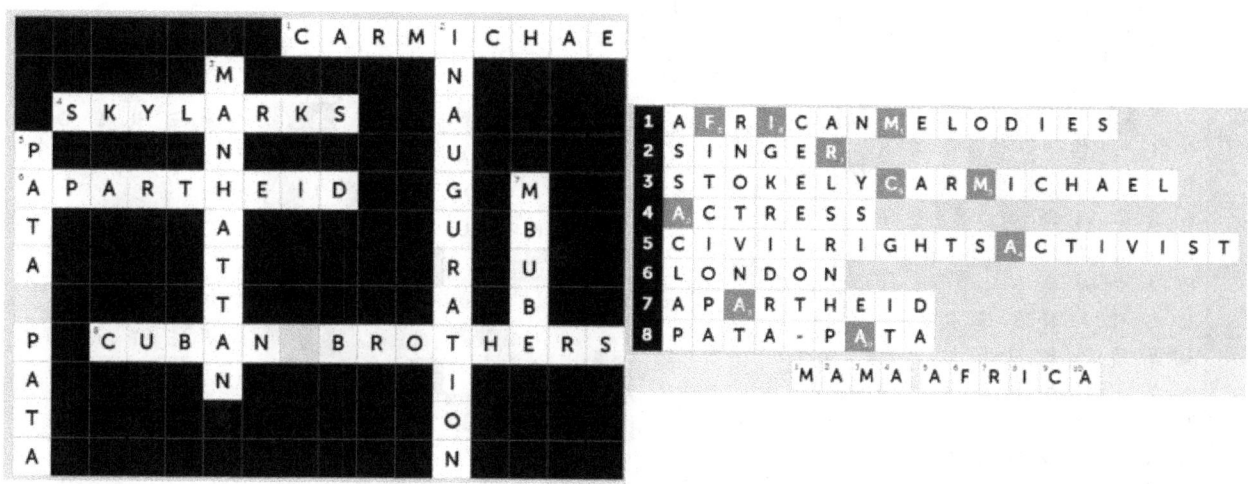

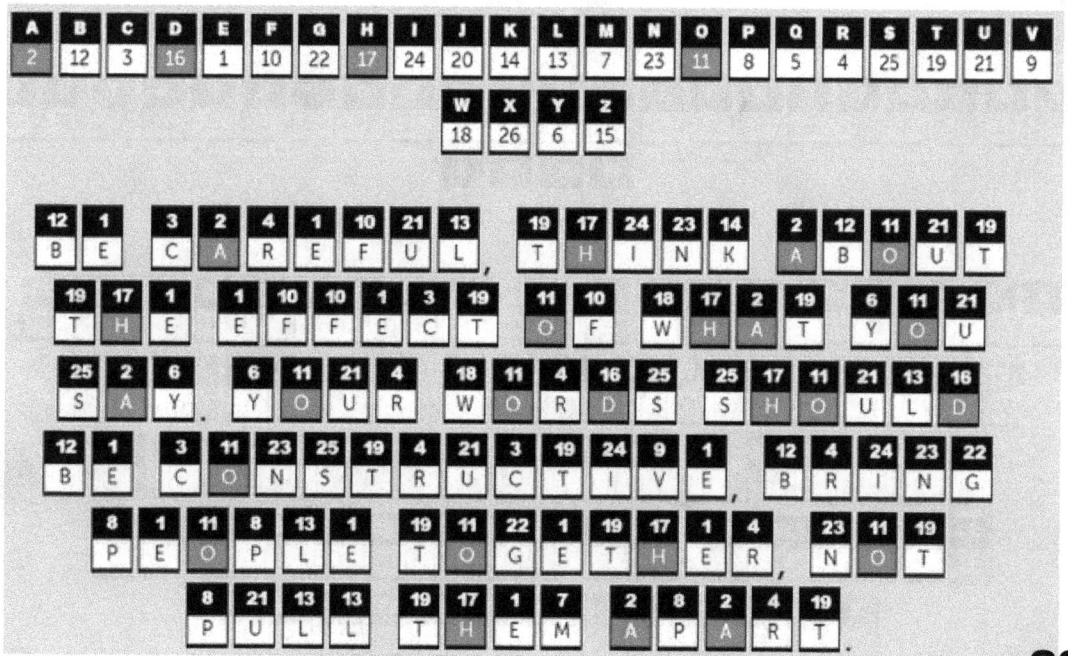

BE CAREFUL, THINK ABOUT THE EFFECT OF WHAT YOU SAY. YOUR WORDS SHOULD BE CONSTRUCTIVE, BRING PEOPLE TOGETHER, NOT PULL THEM APART.

225

Marian Anderson
Answers

1. What song is not one of mine?
   A. Deep River
   B. My Ways Cloudy
   C. Caravan
2. What age did I start doing solo acts?
   A. 6
   B. 10
   C. 21
3. What policy denied me permission for a concert?
   A. Crowd size policy
   B. White performers-only policy
   C. Bag policy

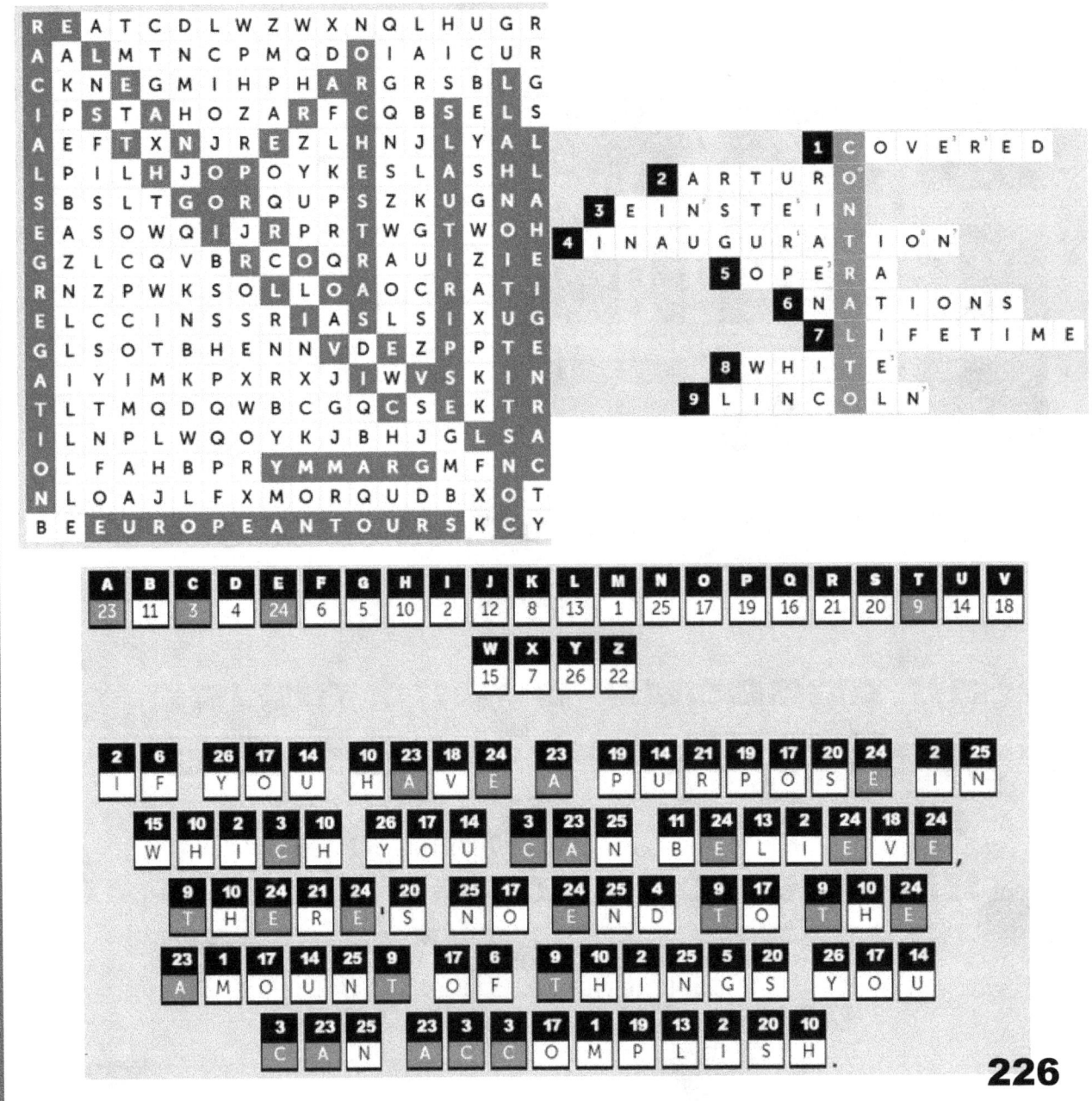

1. COVERED
2. ARTURO
3. EINSTEIN
4. INAUGURATION
5. OPERA
6. NATIONS
7. LIFETIME
8. WHITE
9. LINCOLN

"IF YOU HAVE A PURPOSE IN WHICH YOU CAN BELIEVE, THERE'S NO END TO THE AMOUNT OF THINGS YOU CAN ACCOMPLISH."

226

1. How old was I when I got discovered?
   A. 14
   B. 17
   C. 15
2. What year did I release my first album?
   A. 2005
   B. 2006
   C. 2003
3. What is the name of the record label that signed me?
   A. Arista Records
   B. Def Jam Records
   C. Priority Records

Robyn Rihanna Fenty

Answers

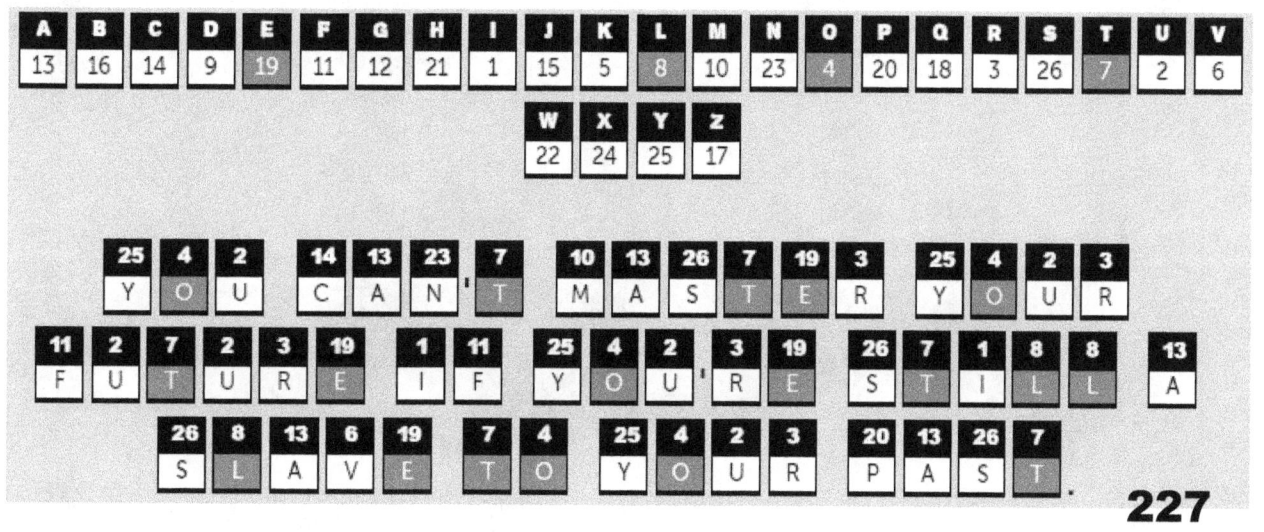

This book is dedicated to my grandkids
Anais Isabella Pablo-Antonio
Deyshawn Frank Chambers
Alicia Marie Jackson
Ayianna Marie Chambers
Zion Jamaris Jackson
Jayvon Jerome Jackson

ABOUT THE AUTHOR

Matthew D. Hale, the author of Black Historical Figures is a retired Marine and disabled veteran. He received his Bachelor of Arts in Computer Science from Campbell University and his Master of Science in Computer Engineering from Boston University. Matthew spends his down time making music, traveling, playing, and developing his own video games. Follow Matthew on Facebook/Meta at wegonnalearntoday, Instagram @ w_g_l_t and Tic Tok at wegonnalearntoday. Go to wegonnalearntoday.com or everydollarcountz.com for additional information.

In 2020 Matthew developed an interactive website, www.wegonnalearntoday, to provide access to Black History through games, music and videos. The website grew into the Black Historical Figures workbook series as a way to supplement the black history curricula taught in the school systems.

'In order to grow you must visit uncomfortable places'

10 BOOK SERIES
RELEASE DATES

NOVEMBER 2022

DECEMBER 2022

MAY 2023

AUGUST 2023

NOVEMBER 2023

GET YOUR COPY TODAY
DON'T FORGET TO TELL A FRIEND

www.ingramcontent.com/pod-product-compliance
Lightning Source LLC
Chambersburg PA
CBHW080335170426
43194CB00014B/2571